JACK NICHOLSON

JACK NICHOLSON

NANCY CAMPBELL

This edition published in 1994 by SMITHMARK Publishers Inc., 16 East 32nd Street, New York, New York 10016

SMITHMARK books are available for bulk purchase for sales promotion and premium use. For details write or telephone the Manager of Special Sales, SMITHMARK Publishers Inc., 16 East 32nd Street, New York, NY 10016. (212) 532-6600.

Produced by Brompton Books Corp., 15 Sherwood Place Greenwich, CT 06830

ISBN 0-8317-5250-5

Printed in China

10 9 8 7 6 5 4 3 2 1

Page 1: Jack's over-the-top performance as the Joker in *Batman* delighted the critics, and is thought to have earned him $60 million. He simply outcamped the film's putative hero, played by Michael Keaton.

Pages 2-3: A scene from *Easy Rider* – the ultimate biker movie – which made Jack an overnight success in 1969. Ironically, he had been reluctant to take on the role of alcoholic Southern lawyer George Hanson. Yet in the end his performance was nominated for an Oscar. In this picture Jack is riding pillion behind Peter Fonda. On the other bike is Dennis Hopper.

These pages: By 1978 Jack was already a major star, with an Oscar for *One Flew Over The Cuckoo's Nest* behind him, but he hankered for success as a director. This was to elude him again with the rather dismal comic Western, *Goin' South*. But it provided a big break for his co-star, Mary Steenburgen.

CONTENTS

PROLOGUE

He is, quite simply, the most contradictory and fascinating movie star ever seen in Hollywood. Open and honest to a fault, he nevertheless remains an enigma. The scourge of feminists, he is adored by women the world over, women who wax lyrical about his 'cobra eyes' and his 'killer smile.' Even the women he has loved, and often treated badly, seem unable to stay mad at him for long. He is only 5ft 10ins tall, with a receding hairline and a potbelly, yet many have described him as the sexiest man alive. According to him, 'if you think you're attractive, you *are* attractive.' Perhaps that's his secret. He says that he has the utmost respect for women, yet often talks about them as if they were mere sex objects. The uncompromising anti-heroes he has played during the last four decades have also won him male fans. He is intelligent, and only wishes to be associated with film roles that stretch him creatively, yet he has often chosen badly. He says money is relatively unimportant, but doesn't miss a trick when negotiating his fee. He has also been known to ring around Europe to ask if a girlfriend has borrowed his comb, rather than buy another one. He is worth in excess of $100 million, but lives in a two-story house that cost him $800,000. He has a pool of cars, including two Mercedes, yet prefers to drive a battered V.W. His friends, however, testify to his generosity and loyalty. He scorns all plaudits yet revels in the glamour of his success, and hones and polishes every performance with one eye on the Oscars. Born out of wedlock, he often bemoans the misfortune of illegitimate children, yet he has not married the mothers of three of his children. He is a law unto himself, he is Jack Nicholson.

Left: A scene from Jack's thirty-eighth movie, *The Postman Always Rings Twice*, with co-star Jessica Lange. By now, Jack was keen to cash in on the wickedly sexy image he had acquired in *Carnal Knowledge*, and his kitchen-table scene with Lange was to become one of his most memorable. The film was a raunchy remake of the original, which had starred John Garfield and Lana Turner.

Right: Jack, who has always professed to scorn accolades, was nevertheless thrilled to win a Best Actor Oscar for *One Flew Over The Cuckoo's Nest*. 'I guess this proves there are as many nuts in the Academy as anywhere else,' he said as he collected the award in 1976.

CHILDHOOD DAYS

'I became conscious of very early emotions of not being wanted; feeling that I was a problem to my family as an infant' – Jack Nicholson

To the casual onlooker there was nothing very out of the ordinary about the Nicholson household on Fifth Avenue in Neptune City, a neat and self-conscious suburb for the aspirational lower middle classes of Neptune, New Jersey.

It was a one-parent family, but that in itself was not unusual, even back in the early 1940s; Ethel May Nicholson had struggled to build up the beauty business she had opened in a back room to help support her children: two girls, June and Lorraine, and a much younger son with a raffish grin and a dreamer's temperament, known then as John.

Ethel May was born into a wealthy Dutch Protestant family in Pennsylvania, which had disinherited her when she ran off to marry John Nicholson, a handsome Irish Catholic. He was a sign painter and window dresser and something of a dandy, remembered by many as one of the best-dressed men at the annual Ashbury Park Easter Parade. Things had gone well for a while: John's pay was meager, but he was a good provider at first, until he started to stay out later and later, holding court in bars and pool halls and invariably arriving home too drunk to stand. Ethel May had thrown him out even before the birth of their son on 22 April 1937. Those were hard times. Europe was on the verge of chaos as Hitler seized power in Germany, and America was still feeling the effects of the Depression. Still, Ethel May was made of stern stuff and, when she heard of a company selling permanent-wave machines, she bought one immediately and opened a beauty parlor in her living room. It wasn't long before she was able to move her family upmarket, to Fifth Avenue.

If Ethel May felt the strain, she didn't let it show. Neither did she breathe a word about what, in those days, would still have been regarded as a scandalous family secret . . . that John wasn't her son at all, but had been born out of wedlock to June when she was 17. John Nicholson Jr. did not discover the truth until he was almost 38 and had become one of the biggest stars in Hollywood. The story was broken to him by *Time* magazine. Dumbstruck, he rang his 'sister,' Lorraine – the only surviving member of his family by then – who confirmed what he had been told. *Time* honored his request to suppress the story and it remained a secret of sorts until the *National Enquirer* ran a piece in 1980, by a man named Don Furcillo Rose, a one-time Italian band singer, who claimed to be Jack's real father, under the headline 'Jack Nicholson's Bizarre Family Secret.'

Whether children raised in families with secrets still sense, in some vague way, that all is not as it seems, is hard to say. But, eerily, years before he learned that his 'sister' June was really his mother, Jack had told interviewers of a strange feeling he had had while experimenting with L.S.D. 'I became,' he recalled, 'conscious of very early emotions of not being wanted; feeling that I was a problem to my family as an infant.' The revelations may at least explain why this renowned libertarian is against abortion to this day. 'I have no right to think any other way,' he told reporters as recently as 1990.

Despite all this, Jack has always insisted that his childhood was happy. 'I was never an underprivileged kid. My mother [grandmother] was a very strong, independent lady who made her own living. I never felt poor, quite the opposite.' For the early part of his life he was surrounded by women and the trappings of femininity in the beauty parlor – hair dryers, the acrid smell of bleaches and perm solutions. He was also privy to their often earthy conversations. No wonder he attributes his success with women to his ability to understand them. The all-female regime at home changed when Lorraine married a railroad brakeman, George Smith. At around the same time, when Jack was four years old, June, whom he later remembered as being 'a symbol of excitement; thrilling and beautiful,' left to join the Earl Carroll dancers in New York.

There apparently followed a spate of spectacular temper tantrums and attention-seeking antics, but Jack soon learned that charm was a more reliable way to get the attention he craved. He was well-liked and easygoing, but there was little to mark him out from his fellow pupils at Roosevelt Grammar School. As he said: 'I enjoyed school but I wasn't into learning. I met the requirements in order to enjoy what I liked most about

Right: Jack in typical 'lady-killer' pose – arching his eyebrows and flashing those famous 'cobra' eyes. Candice Bergen had been telling the world about them since they appeared together in *Carnal Knowledge*.

Left: An early family portrait showing, from left: Ethel May – the woman Jack believed was his mother until he was almost 38 – a family friend, the young Jack and his real mother, June, whom he had grown up believing was his sister. The photograph was taken on one of the family's regular trips to Bradley Beach, New Jersey.

school – being around lots of people and having a good time.' He made his stage debut at the age of 10, giving a forgettable rendition of a popular song of the time, *Managua, Nicaragua.*

For a while Jack's summers were punctuated by holidays on Long Island with June and her children – whom he believed were his nieces and nephews – from her marriage to a wealthy East Coast surgeon. But the marriage soon failed and June moved back to Neptune, commuting to New York where she taught dancing at Arthur Murray's. It would not be long before she would take the path Jack would later follow, and head off to find fame and fortune in Hollywood.

As a teenager Jack grew chubby – the result of bingeing on junk food, an addiction he admits to this day. He kept up contact with his 'father,' John, recalling: 'He was an incredible drinker. I would drink about 18 sarsaparillas while he'd have 35 shots of three-star Hennessy . . . But I never heard him raise his voice; I never saw anybody angry with him. He was just a quiet, melancholy, tragic figure – a very soft man.' Old schoolfriends remember Jack saying: 'I saw my father yesterday. The poor guy; I feel sorry for him because he can't help it.' Pity, however, is not the noblest of emotions, and when John died in 1958 Jack missed the funeral because he didn't want to leave Hollywood.

Ethel, meanwhile, was a tolerant 'mother' and Jack had a free rein: 'I was the only kid who never HAD to go home, as long as I called to let her know I was all right.' She kept a 'penny jar' in the hallway, which he plundered to go to the movies and to buy books. By now Ethel had moved the family upmarket again, to 505 Mercer Avenue in Spring Lake, a resort community a few miles south of Neptune.

Jack was a pupil at Manasguan High School, although not, he'd be the first to admit, an illustrious one. Naturally bright, he could get good marks with little effort, but had what he later described as 'deportment problems.' He was suspended three times: for swearing, smoking and vandalism. The last offense was the

Left: Even up until 1992 Don Furcillo Rose was telling anyone who would listen how desperately he wanted to see his son, Jack Nicholson. The two had spoken by telephone, but had never met. Don always claimed to have secretly wed June, only to be banned from seeing her again by Ethel May.

Left: Jack, at 24, looking deceptively innocent in a publicity photograph from *Studs Lonigan.* He had a small role as a member of Studs' gang, but was thrilled to be working for a major studio, United Artists.

most serious. A keen sports enthusiast, Jack played freshman football, and later managed the varsity baseball team. On one occasion he was so angry after a game that he sneaked into the opposing team's gymnasium and wrecked the electronic switchboard. As a result he was banned from school sports and was required to take odd jobs to pay for the damage. For a while he was a caddie at a local country club; later he was a lifeguard at Bradley Beach.

Jack's contradictory personality is perhaps best summed up by the fact that one year he was voted both Class Optimist and Class Pessimist. He also won awards for his acting – and for his clowning – in the school drama classes. He graduated in 1954, aged 17. After considering college and a career in journalism or chemical engineering, and after being offered financial assistance, Jack decided that he was destined for greater things. He wasn't quite sure what, but he had a hunch that he would find the answer if he went to stay with June in Hollywood.

LEARNING HIS CRAFT

'There are two ways up the ladder: hand over hand, or scratching and clawing. It sure has been tough on my nails' – Jack Nicholson

By the time Jack Nicholson became an 'overnight success' in 1969, aged 32, he had appeared in 20 films, had written or co-written six, and had helped edit or direct five, most of them for legendary cult B-movie producer, Roger Corman.

His quest for fame had begun the day he arrived on June's doorstep in Inglewood, Los Angeles, a suburb about 10 miles from Hollywood. She had given up show business and was now working as a secretary in an aircraft factory; later she became a buyer for the department-store chain, J.C. Penney. Even from 10 miles away the glamour of Hollywood was infectious. On young Jack's arrival one of his idols, James Dean, was making *East of Eden*; another, Marlon Brando, had just finished filming *On The Waterfront*.

For six months Jack drifted around at the local race track and pool halls, and was about to return to New Jersey when he landed a job as an office boy and messenger in the mail room of the animation department at M.G.M. in nearby Culver City. His principal responsibility was handling fan letters to Tom and Jerry.

His salary was $30 a week, which didn't leave much once he had paid the rent on the bachelor apartment he had taken. He enjoyed his job but was otherwise depressed – and lonely. 'I'd never been anywhere where I didn't know everybody. I had no friends. It was only a couple of months, but it seemed like 90 years before I got to know some people,' he later recalled. The old-style studio system was in its death throes; young actors were not being taken on on contract, and even once-famous veterans were on welfare as the movie industry was plunged into recession by the emergence of T.V. Still, on a good day at M.G.M. you could still close your eyes and dream – and, if you were

Previous pages: In *Hell's Angels On Wheels*, Jack played a gas-station attendant who quits his job, tempted by life on the road with a gang of Hell's Angels. It was a blatant exploitation movie based on *The Wild Angels*, a European cult hit for Peter Fonda. Both films preceded *Easy Rider*.

Left and far left: Two scenes from *Studs Lonigan* – the movie for which Jack had such high hopes in 1960; although the film was based on a celebrated novel, it was not a box-office draw.

Above: Cry Baby Killer was Jack's first big break in 1957, made by Roger Corman to cash in on the success of *Rebel Without A Cause* with James Dean. Like Dean, Jack played a confused adolescent.

Right: A scene from *Back Door To Hell*, a badly-written World War II drama. 'People who haven't seen my early movies are better off than I am but, like all actors, I needed the work. I did these movies because they were the only work I could get,' said Jack.

Below: In 1961 Jack starred with Diana Darrin in *The Broken Land*, a dire pseudopsychological Western, again by Roger Corman.

Above: In *The Terror*, another Roger Corman project which was thrown together over a weekend, Jack played a Napoleonic officer and starred with veteran horror-movie actor, Boris Karloff. Both actors still owed Corman two days' work after appearing in *The Raven* with Vincent Price and Peter Lorre.

lucky, you might steal a glimpse of Grace Kelly, Lana Turner or Rita Moreno.

Jack's small-town ways won him friends easily around the studio. He would greet even the industry's bigwigs by their first names – and get away with it. He got his first screen test simply by asking for it on a chance encounter with star-maker producer Joe Pasternak. For all his nerve he failed the test. But, ever the optimist, he was not dispirited. After all, if someone like Pasternak had seen enough potential in him to arrange the test, then maybe he really did have something. With the help of Tom and Jerry's creators, Bill Hanna and Joe Barbera, he persuaded M.G.M.'s talent scouts to get him an apprenticeship at the West Coast's most prestigious showcase for young actors, the Player's Ring Theater. Jack also joined an acting class run by Jeff Corey. Fellow students included actors James Coburn and Sally Kellerman, writers Carol Eastman (who would write one of Jack's most successful films, *Five Easy Pieces*), Robert Towne (later responsible for *The Last Detail, Chinatown* and *The Two Jakes*) and John Shaner (future writer of *Goin' South*). There was also a young producer named Roger Corman. These people became a surrogate family to Jack. But Jeff Corey was unimpressed by his work, telling him that it had 'no poetry.' 'Perhaps you're not seeing the poetry I'm showing you,' snarled Jack.

In early July 1955, when Jack had just turned 19,

John Nicholson died of a heart condition and cancer of the colon. Jack sent his condolences but decided against flying back for the funeral in New Jersey. He was genuinely broke and, besides, his social life had taken off in a big way – so much so that he decided to quit his job at M.G.M. and draw welfare checks, a decision which worried June.

However, long before Bob Dylan penned his words, the times were indeed a-changing. Los Angeles was suddenly teeming with youthful artists – the Beat Generation – who spent their evenings in the dozens of coffee houses that had opened up to cater for these intense young people who were going to change the world. Here they would sit in their turtleneck sweaters, with unkempt hair, talking earnestly into the early hours about the meaning of life and Zen Buddhism – actors, painters, poets, sculptors, musicians and folk singers, all followers of Sartre, Camus, Kierkegaard and, of course, *On The Road* author Jack Kerouac. Jack Nicholson was a regular at the first beatnik coffee house, the Unicorn on Sunset Strip; there were also the Renaissance, the Sea Witch and Chez Paulette, and he used to try to steal a glimpse of his idol, Brando, who was dating a waitress at the more upmarket Cosmos Alley. His favorite, however, was the Raincheck on Sunset Boulevard, a few doors from the Player's Ring.

After James Dean died when he crashed his Porsche in 1955, the young actors dared each other to do 'numbers' (outrageous acts to prove how crazy they were). Craziness was very 'hip' at the time, and few participants were more 'hip' than Jack. He did a 'number' when, in a mock rage, he swept aside dishes, glasses and cutlery from a table in Pupi's, a coffee house on the Strip (he later drew on this memory for a similar scene in *Five Easy Pieces*). After cruising the coffee houses all evening, they would invariably end up at the Sea Witch, which broadcast late-night radio, before wrapping it up at Canter's, a delicatessen on Fairfax Avenue. Sometimes they would congregate at Samson DeBrier's, a movie aficionado whose house was an open salon, cluttered with movie props and autographed photographs. It was at DeBrier's that Jack had been introduced to – and snubbed by – James Dean in early 1955.

Marijuana was the drug of the moment. Old acquaintances allege that Jack seemed stoned more often than not. 'It was as though someone would come in with this Jack Nicholson mannequin and set it down in the booth at Schwab's [an afternoon drugstore and coffee house on the Strip] and it would just sit there, smiling,' recalled movie-business player, John Gilmore.

Then, of course, there were the women. Jack's famous libido was insatiable. He has often claimed that he went into acting because it was a good way to meet the prettiest girls, or 'chicks,' as he still refers to women. Sometimes the crowd would move on to a private house on Melrose Avenue where orgies were held. There were usually about 12 participants – and

several times as many voyeurs. Jack was never seen joining in; he would just sit there, grinning inanely. Nevertheless, when, with his usual candor, he mentioned these orgies in passing years later, it proved a field day for the press.

Most days Jack would stay in bed until 3-4 pm, and would then drag himself sleepily down to Schwab's, or Barney's Beano on Santa Monica Boulevard. He was still fitting in his acting classes, of course, but for a while he seemed content simply to have a good time. According to John Gilmore he was seen as a bit of a joke: 'I don't care who claims now to have seen potential in him; the fact is no one took him seriously then.' Jack himself insists that he was always serious about acting, and remembers stealing wood from lumberyards, toilets from old gas stations, and so on, to equip the Stage Theater, an experimental theater on Santa Monica Boulevard.

His big break finally came in 1957, when he won the lead role in *Cry Baby Killer*, a typical exploitation movie by Roger Corman, which tried to cash in on the hysteria created by *Rebel Without A Cause*. 'I said to myself "This is it!"' recalled Jack. He played Jimmy Walker, a mixed-up teenager who is attacked by three toughs at a drive-in restaurant. He picks up a gun and fires at two of the gang. Thinking he has killed them, he holds hostages under siege in a nearby restaurant. His girlfriend, shouting from behind police lines with a megaphone, persuades him that he has killed no one, and that she still loves him, so he surrenders. The movie was shot in 10 days and cost $7000 to make. The critics panned it, one dismissing the 'vapid mob voyeurism' to which it pandered. After this Jack didn't work again for many months until he made his stage debut in *Tea And Sympathy* at the Player's Ring. The cast included Michael Landon, who went on to find fame in the television series, *Bonanza*. Indeed, one by one, all the other actors were offered T.V. work, but Jack had to wait several months before being offered bit parts in daytime T.V. shows like *Divorce Court* and *Matinée Theater*.

In 1959 Jack's luck changed when he landed four movies – all released in 1960. In *Too Soon To Love* he played the friend of a young man who gets his girlfriend pregnant; in *The Wild Ride* he played a ruthless road-gang leader who causes several fatal crashes – both movies were for Corman. He pinned much hope on *Studs Lonigan*. Although he only had a bit part as one of Studs' gang, it was his debut performance with a major studio, United Artists. Sadly, the film vanished almost without trace. Indeed, the only early movie that showed Jack's potential was *The Little Shop Of Horrors*, which was remade as a multimillion-dollar musical by Warner Brothers in 1984. In this movie, Jack played Wilber Force, the masochistic patient of a sadistic dentist. 'This is going to hurt you more than it's going to hurt me,' leers the dentist; 'No Novocaine; it dulls the senses,' replies Jack. As the drilling starts he cries 'Oh my God, don't stop now,' and, at the end, 'I can truly say I've never enjoyed myself so much.' Movie buffs still regard this performance as vintage Jack Nicholson.

There followed another lull. Jack dropped out of Jeff Corey's acting classes to study 'The Method' with

Left: Heavily into the drug culture of the 1960s, Jack wrote *The Trip* for Roger Corman and was miffed when the lead role went to Peter Fonda. He hated the way it was cut, and Fonda later said that, in its original form, it could have been 'the greatest film ever made in America.'

Right: Always attracted to Westerns, Jack starred in *The Shooting*, written by acting-class friend from the old days, Carol Eastman. Here, as Billy Spear, he threatens Coley, played by Will Hutchins.

Martin Landau, and the partying, the 'chicks' and the pot-smoking took over again. By now he was renting a house with writer-to-be Don Devlin and producer-in-waiting Harry Gittes on Fountain Avenue, a few streets from Sunset Boulevard; Jack described it as 'the wildest house in Hollywood.' He had also started a more serious relationship with a young actress he had met in Landau's class: Sandra Knight was auburn-haired, striking-looking, intelligent and slightly dominant – the perfect foil for someone as wayward as Jack.

Around this time Jack was also called up for military service. Like many antiwar young people, he had earlier joined the Air National Guard, never dreaming that his fire-fighting unit would be called to active duty. But it was, and for a year he had to serve out his time at the Van Nuys facility near Hollywood.

On 17June 1962 Jack married Sandra Knight. Later he would say: 'It was no big deal for me. I got married not thinking about it one way or the other; I just loved the girl.' He was 25, she was 22, and the best man was actor Harry Dean Stanton.

Jack's next film was *The Broken Land*, a pseudo-psychological Western – and another turkey, again for Corman. These days he says of his early career: 'People who haven't seen my early movies are better off than I am but, like all actors, I needed the work. I did these movies because they were the only work I could get.' Clearly worried about his future, Jack joined the William Morris Agency, where he met the man who represents him to this day, Sandy Bresler. Next came another typical Corman parody, *The Raven*, which at least promised the chance to work with veterans like Boris Karloff, Vincent Price and Peter Lorre. It was based loosely – very loosely – on a poem by Edgar Allan Poe. When filming was completed two days ahead of schedule, Corman decided to make full use of the actors' paid time, and the sets, to write and shoot another movie over the weekend, called *The Terror*. Jack played a Napoleonic officer and Sandra played the heroine, Helene.

Both of these films again played to a campus audience. Jack was desperate to be seen in a more prestigious film, and must have thought his chance had come when he was offered an unbilled bit part as a sailor named Dolan in a Warner Brothers project called *Ensign Pulver*, which also boasted a glitzy cast, including Walter Matthau, Burl Ives and Larry Hagman.

Just as he was about to leave for filming in Acapulco, he learned that June (his sister/mother) was dying of cancer. He recalled: 'She looked me right in the eye and said "Shall I wait? Shall I try to fight this through?" And I said "No."' She died the day he left for Mexico.

On the day of his return, Sandra gave birth to a daughter, Jennifer. *Ensign Pulver*, meanwhile, did not live up to expectations and was quickly sold off to T.V. Jack again turned his attentions to co-writing and co-directing a film called *Thunder Island* – a weak story about a Latin American dictator who flees to the Caribbean. Next came *Back Door To Hell*, a badly-written World War II drama, and *Flight To Fury*, which Jack wrote, and which concerned a psychopathic killer's murderous spree as he tries to locate a pouch of

diamonds. Neither movie achieved box-office or critical success. However, Jack was soon on to his next project, co-writing, co-directing and starring in a Western called *Ride The Whirlwind*, again commissioned by Corman. While in the Utah desert he also opportunely starred in another Western, *The Shooting*, written by his old acting-class friend, Carol Eastman. Filming finished in 1965, but when Corman saw the first prints of *Ride The Whirlwind*, he thought it was too esoteric and would never sell. But he agreed to pay for Jack to take it to the Cannes Film Festival, where the European reception was warm, particularly from French director Jean-Luc Godard. A French distributor offered to take it on, but the company went bust before Jack landed back in Los Angeles.

By 1966 Jack was getting desperate. He was nearly 30; his friend, Warren Beatty, had hit the big time already, and was living the millionaire lifestyle and notching up affairs with Natalie Wood and Joan Collins. Jack had fought to test for *The Graduate*, but the role went to another 30-year-old, Dustin Hoffman. He had also tired of marriage – 'the rows bored me' – and Sandra was upset by his occasional infidelities and drug-taking. The pair had, under medical supervision, experimented with L.S.D. Jack found the experience 'enlightening,' despite uncovering his then inexplicable feelings about being unwanted as a baby and a burden to his family. Sandra had had a bad 'trip' and subsequently turned to religion. By the end of the year Sandra had left with Jennifer to live in Hawaii.

The partying started all over again when Jack moved into a house with Harry Dean Stanton in Laurel Canyon. He was now filming *Hell's Angels On Wheels*, an exploitation movie based on a film called *The Wild Angels*, starring Peter Fonda and Bruce Dern, which had become a cult hit in Europe. Jack played a gas-station attendant who quits his job to go on the road with a gang of Hell's Angels.

In his private life he also began an affair with a beautiful model who had a bit part in the movie, named Mimi Machu. Next, through Bruce Dern, he took a small role in *Rebel Rousers*. This was quickly followed by *The St Valentine's Day Massacre*, in which Jack had one line of 12 words, but at least he was starring alongside Jason Robards Jr., George Segal and Bruce Dern.

At this time the drugs culture was in full swing. Dr. Timothy Leary was inviting people to 'tune in, turn on and drop out' and, on the back of this, Jack began writing *Psych-Out*, a movie about hippiedom in the Haight-Ashbury district of San Francisco. Staying on the drugs theme, he also wrote *The Trip*, about a T.V. commercial director facing separation from his wife and disillusioned by the commercialism of his profession. To Jack's chagrin, Corman toned down the script and refused to offer him an acting role in the film, opting instead for names like Peter Fonda, Susan Strasberg, Dennis Hopper and Bruce Dern. Still more cuts were demanded by the distributors, who feared that it would appear to condone drug-taking. When Jack saw the final version he hated it; indeed, even Peter Fonda would say later that, in its original form, *The Trip* could

Left: Jack and Peter Fonda in a scene from *Easy Rider.* Jack had been persuaded to join the cast at the last moment by Bob Rafelson. Rafelson, who had put up $375,000 of his own money, was worried by the on-set antics of Fonda and director Dennis Hopper.

have been 'the greatest film ever made in America.'

Just when he was seriously thinking of quitting Hollywood, Jack met up with Bob Rafelson and Bert Schneider, who were marketing The Monkees, America's answer to The Beatles. Inspired by *A Hard Day's Night*, they asked Jack to write a script for the band. The result was *Head*, a surreal effort which featured footage of cowboys and Indians, the Vietnam War, and fading star Victor Mature as the Jolly Green Giant. The *New York Times* called it 'a dreadfully-written script'; Jack loved it, but it put an end to The Monkees' career.

By now Jack had become friendly with film director Roman Polanski, who was then making *Rosemary's Baby.* Jack pleaded for the role of Rosemary's husband, but Polanski refused, explaining: 'For all his talent, his faintly sinister appearance ruled him out. The part called for a clean-cut, conventional actor.' The part eventually went to John Cassavetes.

Jack was in the pre-production stage of a movie he was to direct and star in, called *Drive, He Said*, when Bob Rafelson asked him to try to rescue a biking film that had run into trouble in the hands of Dennis Hopper and Peter Fonda. The two had been running around for months with $375,000 of Rafelson's money, shooting everything that moved. Rafelson wanted Jack to replace Rip Torn (who had walked out) as the disenchanted alcoholic Southern lawyer, George Hanson. The film was called *Easy Rider.* To say that Jack was reluctant is an understatement, but he felt he owed Rafelson. Inevitably he joined in the chaos. During the famous campfire scene he and Hopper allegedly smoked over 100 joints. This was fine at first, when the script called for them to get gradually stoned, but as they reshot the opening lines, they found they were required to act normally when they could hardly stand. Another time, after an off-screen session with Hopper, Jack awoke to find himself up a tree alone, with no recollection of getting there: 'It was just a crazy experience from beginning to end,' remembered Jack.

Even before the film was released there was a buzz in Hollywood. Against all the odds, the gossip went, Fonda and Hopper had managed to create an outstanding movie, perhaps largely due to the brilliant cinematography of Laszlo Kovacs. And, rumor had it, there was a very promising young actor in it, by the name of Jack Nicholson. Within days of its release, *Easy Rider* was being hailed as a classic. It would eventually take $45 million. Jack was nominated for an Oscar as Best Supporting Actor, but lost out to Gig Young for *They Shoot Horses Don't They?*

Jack was now the toast of Cannes. The first time he had visited the festival it was as an unknown trying to hustle for a deal. Now, aged 32, he had finally made the major league. As he recalled: 'I'm one of the few people who was actually present at the moment I became a star. I mean, I could actually sense it in the audience.' Little could he have known then, however, that this was just the beginning of a career that would see him eclipse most of the friends who had succeeded before him. Or that it would buy him a house right next door to Marlon Brando.

FROM *EASY RIDER* TO *CHINATOWN*

Previous pages: Jack with Dennis Hopper in *Easy Rider*. Hopper had a reputation in Hollywood of being difficult but, to some extent, he redeemed himself with the huge financial success of *Easy Rider*.

Below: The cast of *Easy Rider* – Hopper far left, Fonda center and Jack far right – formed the craziest chorus line ever seen at the Cannes Film Festival as they promoted the film.

Right: The infamous campfire scene from *Easy Rider* with, from left, Fonda, Jack and Hopper. Jack and Hopper allegedly smoked over 100 joints while filming this scene. 'It was just a crazy experience from beginning to end,' recalled Jack.

'Like most people I just drifted into acting. It was the best goddam piece of drifting I ever did' – Jack Nicholson

At around the same time as Jack Nicholson was finding fame and acclaim at Cannes, a macabre drama was being played out in Los Angeles. One morning in August 1969 Hollywood woke up to the grisly details of the Manson murders, a mass slaughter so gruesome that it would signal the end of the sex-and-drugs-and-rock-and-roll counterculture personified in films like *Easy Rider*. Jack's most famous line in the film: 'This used to be a helluva good country' seemed, unwittingly, to sum it up. Self-styled 'messiah' Charles Manson and his disciples had crept into a Beverly Hills compound and butchered everyone in sight. Five people died, including an 18-year-old boy, who had merely been visiting the caretaker, and the heavily-pregnant Sharon Tate, wife of controversial film director Roman Polanski.

Although Jack was only on the periphery of this tragedy, he got caught up in its backwash. His friendship with Polanski was only in its early stages – Polanski claims to have introduced Jack to the joys of skiing – but he felt compelled to rally to his defense when some sections of the media chose to portray the killings as in

some way 'deserved,' because some of the victims had experimented with drugs and kinky sex. Years later, when Polanski fled the U.S. following charges of having had sex with an underage girl in Jack's home, Jack said: 'His situation is a very interesting case of what notoriety can do to you. I always felt that Roman was exiled because his wife had the bad taste to be murdered in the newspapers . . . ' The irony was lost on many, who thought that he was somehow condoning Polanski's behavior. He wasn't, but he may have felt that Polanski didn't deserve to be judged by people who could scarcely comprehend the ordeal his friend had suffered. He attended each day of the Manson trial, saying he 'just wanted to see' for himself, as if he could hardly believe what had happened. As a final irony, when Manson was being courted later to sell the film rights to his twisted life, he asked that the film be made by the team behind *Easy Rider*.

Jack, however, had other things on his mind. Though he failed to win an Oscar for *Easy Rider*, he was chosen as Best Actor by the influential New York Critics' Circle.

He had also stretched himself to buy the home of his dreams, a two-story, eight-roomed house on star-studded Mulholland Drive, with spectacular views over the San Fernando Valley; he shared the entrance with Marlon Brando. There was a den with a wall-sized T.V. and a wooden deck with a pool; Jack had a balcony added with a gate set in it, so that he could walk out of the master bedroom and jump straight into the pool. He also started to collect art (he was later named by a U.S. magazine as one of the top 60 collectors in America). His taste, not surprisingly, covered Picasso, Magritte, Matisse and de Lempica. He also installed a library – reading was one of his passions. His eclectic taste also showed in his record collection, from The Rolling Stones to Rimsky-Korsakov. A Mercedes 600 was parked ostentatiously in the drive, although he still preferred to use his battered old V.W.

Jack's next film project was different, to say the least, and would prove to be the first of many ill-advised decisions he would make in his early years of stardom. He was invited to play a hippie in a new Barbra Streisand

vehicle, to be directed by Vincente Minnelli. Like Minnelli's most successful films, this was to be a musical, and Jack had to sing a duet with Streisand. The film was to be called *On A Clear Day You Can See Forever*. By way of explanation Jack said: 'If I hadn't broken from it right at the beginning they wouldn't have let me play anything but *Easy Rider*.' He was flattered to be asked by Minnelli; former Vogue editor Diana Vreeland said that Jack was 'easily seduced by anything that suggests the possibility of something grand.' If he started to worry when the costume department cut his hair short and clothed him in rollnecks, casual trousers and sports jackets, he was too professional to say so. He also had precious little contact with Minnelli: 'You sort of have to guess what he wants,' said Jack. In the event his sitar-strumming duet with Streisand was left on the cutting-room floor, and the woefully old-fashioned film was quietly ignored, except by the critic who commented that Jack's 'miniscule' part was 'a giant step backward from *Easy Rider*.'

Jack's next film held more promise. He had returned to the safety of Bob Rafelson and Bert Schneider who, by now, had also taken a third partner, Steve Blauner, and had become B.B.S. Productions, with a finance and distribution deal with Columbia. *Five Easy Pieces* was scripted by another old friend, Carol Eastman, and was to be directed by Rafelson and photographed by

Top: Jack starred with Karen Black in *Five Easy Pieces*, again written by Carol Eastman. Black talked about having fallen in love with Jack, although he was still technically with model Mimi Machu.

Above: Another actress, Susan Anspach, also had a part in *Five Easy Pieces*. Jack and Anspach had an affair during filming which resulted in a child, Caleb.

Right: As Bobby Dupea in *Five Easy Pieces*, Jack played a gifted pianist who spurns his middle-class family's aspirations to become an oil-rigger in the Mojave Desert.

Right: Jack pictured with Art Garfunkel in a scene from *Carnal Knowledge*, directed by Mike Nichols. His role, as the chauvinistic Jonathan, was to become his most controversial yet. Being sexually explicit, the movie angered feminists, divided the critics, and was banned as 'pornographic' in the State of Georgia.

Laszlo Kovacs, the man credited with creating the mood on *Easy Rider*. Jack played Bobby Dupea, a gifted pianist who spurns the expectations of his middle-class musical family to become an oil-rigger in the Mojave Desert. He and Rafelson fell out over a scene where Jack had to break down and confront his dying father about his rebelliousness and drifting lifestyle. Rafelson wanted Dupea to cry; Jack felt that a man like Dupea would never lose his composure like that. Eventually Rafelson accused Jack of not wanting to do it because he couldn't do it. The result was one of the most explosively emotional scenes in Jack's career, and helped him win a second Oscar nomination for Best Actor.

Co-star Karen Black revealed later that she had fallen in love with Jack during filming, but that they had 'never got it together.' Little did she know then that although officially he was still with Mimi, he had had an affair – which lasted only as long as the filming did – with another actress in the cast, Susan Anspach. Nine months later Susan would give birth to Jack's child, a son named Caleb. He also befriended another actress, Helen Kallianiotes, who later moved into Mulholland Drive as his 'totally platonic' personal assistant and cook when her marriage hit the rocks. She was there when Mimi eventually left him, citing his unfaithfulness, drug-taking, possessiveness and bleak Irish moods. For all his philandering, Jack was devastated: 'I had been with her for three years, in love. After she left I couldn't even hear her name mentioned without breaking out into a cold sweat,' he admitted. He sought refuge with his old friend, Harry Dean Stanton: 'He was almost incoherent. I've never seen such despair,' recalled Stanton. Jack then decided to go into Reichian therapy, feeling he had driven Mimi away because ever since his divorce from Sandra Knight he had become a 'walking cliché' of the predatory male.

In public Jack was putting a brave face on things. He was thrilled to attend the Oscars ceremony: 'I love them. I'm very Fifties Zen – all tributes are false vanity – but it's fun. I've been following these things since I was a kid. And I've always had a better time when I know I'm not going to win, because then I'm just Mr. Hollywood.' He was right about not winning: the award went to George C. Scott for *Patton*.

Jack still hankered after directing, and was soon doing just that on another B.B.S. project, *Drive, He Said*.

It was a small-budget movie, only $800,000, and although he cast rising stars Karen Black and Bruce Dern, nothing could save this already dated story of campus unrest set against the Vietnam War. He was also on a very tight schedule because he had signed up for Mike Nichols' new film, *Carnal Knowledge*.

Early in 1970 Ethel May Nicholson, the woman Jack still believed to be his mother, died. He flew to the funeral in New Jersey and asked to be left alone with her at the funeral parlor; he sat beside her casket for more than an hour. He would later often lament the fact that she didn't live to see him win his first Oscar.

In other ways, however, Jack's personal life was picking up. He had met Michelle Phillips, formerly of the singing group, The Mamas and Papas, when she was engaged to his old buddy Dennis Hopper. Hopper's explosive and difficult personality had almost guaranteed that the marriage would fail, which it did after only eight days. She turned to Jack for consolation; he needed consolation too and soon fell helplessly in love again. He wanted Michelle to move in but she, fiercely independent, refused. However, she did agree to move in next door when he offered to buy the adjoining smaller house at Mulholland Drive. His conscience was troubling Jack, though, and he couldn't enjoy his new-found love until he had rung Hopper to make sure it was O.K.

Jack reported for work on *Carnal Knowledge* in spring 1970. Mike Nichols was very much the director of the moment, and had to his credit movies like *Who's Afraid Of Virginia Woolf?* and *The Graduate*. Jack worked for him during the week and spent his weekends editing *Drive, He Said*. He could hardly have guessed that *Carnal Knowledge* would prove his most controversial film so far, and would saddle him with an image he would sometimes regret. The movie spanned 30 years in the lives of two college friends, and co-starred Art Garfunkel (of the group Simon and Garfunkel), Candice Bergen and Ann-Margret. Jack played Jonathan, the archetypal male chauvinist, to whom love is a four-letter word. There were plenty of four-letter words in the script, and also a daring full-frontal shot of Ann-Margret. It was one of the most sexually explicit films since the demise of the foot-on-the-floor Hollywood Production Code.

Upon its release in 1971 *Carnal Knowledge* ran straight into trouble. The critics had mixed feelings about it; the fast-growing women's liberation movement targeted Jack as an enemy on the scale of Norman Mailer and Hugh Hefner; and the film was banned as 'pornographic' in the State of Georgia. This ruling was eventually overturned in the Supreme Court, but by then the damage had been done. At first Jack was hurt: 'You play a character that creates such an impression that suddenly it can change your own life. I didn't editorialize. I was just doing my job and, anyway, it was a legitimate representation of male attitudes at the time. I try to duck conversations about feminism, it's all so dehumanizing . . . ' Within months, however, he seemed to be relishing his new reputation, and was

Left: Here Jack is pictured in another scene from *Carnal Knowledge*, this time with a woman who was not a sexual conquest, but did become a friend – Candice Bergen.

Top: Devastated – but only briefly – after Mimi left, Jack soon fell for Michelle Phillips, formerly of The Mamas and Papas. Michelle (to the left of Jack in this photograph) left Dennis Hopper for Jack but would, in turn, leave Jack for Warren Beatty.

Above: Jack directs an actor in *Drive, He Said*, a small-budget movie which he also co-produced and edited while filming *Carnal Knowledge*. His efforts, however, were jeered at Cannes.

spilling the beans to *Playboy* magazine about his pot-smoking, his attendance at orgies, and a certain sexual problem he had had – to do with overenthusiasm – until he was 26. One of his more interesting revelations was that he had a tendency to be attracted to dominant women whom he would then turn into a 'mother figure,' women who would make him feel 'small and childish' to the extent that he sought to bolster his ego in constant one-night stands. Yet he told other interviewers that he had discovered that he liked 'sharing things,' and that his 'expanding sexuality' was best satisfied not through promiscuity, but by 'continuously communicating with someone specifically.' The damage seemed to have been done, however, and, in a strange repetition of the way she had left Hopper, Michelle left Jack for Warren Beatty.

Again Jack was broken-hearted, but remained philosophical when Michelle rang to ask if he had any feelings about it. 'I thought it was fabulous because I am fond of them both. Michelle is a real stand-up lady, incapable of anything dishonorable,' said a typically magnanimous Jack. To make things worse, *Drive, He Said*, which was released just after *Carnal Knowledge*, ran into trouble with the censors, and was jeered at Cannes. Despite all this, Jack was still very much in demand. He was the first choice for the lead in *The Great Gatsby*, but seemed deliberately to outprice himself, so that the role went to Robert Redford instead. He also turned down the lead in *The Day Of The Jackal*. Perversely, he chose to work with an old friend,

Above: Dumped by Michelle Phillips, berated for *Carnal Knowledge*, scorned for *Drive, He Said*, and forgotten in *A Safe Place*, Jack rushed headlong into another commercial flop, *The King Of Marvin Gardens*. He is seen here in a scene with Bruce Dern.

Right and opposite right: Two further scenes from *The King Of Marvin Gardens* – a mood piece about the relationship between two brothers – directed by Bob Rafelson. Critics complained that it was too downbeat: 'Can you imagine someone saying that to Faulkner? Stop writing all those downbeat stories? No, it's puerile,' raged Jack.

but an untried director, Henry Jaglom, on *A Safe Place* – again for B.B.S. Jack knew it would never be a commercial success, but it offered him the chance to co-star with Orson Welles. Unfortunately the film was released quickly, disappeared almost as quickly – and Jack barely even saw Welles. Next came another obscure choice of movie, again with Bob Rafelson and Laszlo Kovacs. Called *The King Of Marvin Gardens*, it was a mood piece about the relationship between two brothers, which again died a death at the box office. Critics complained about it being too downbeat. 'Can you imagine someone saying that to Faulkner? Stop writing all those downbeat stories? No, it's puerile. Any critic who would say a thing like that is inadequate to his profession,' raged Jack.

He badly needed a break. There was talk of a remake of the film-noir classic, *The Postman Always Rings Twice*, to be renamed *Three-Cornered Circle*. There was even talk of Jack co-starring with Michelle Phillips, but the project collapsed when M.G.M. balked at using Phillips.

Then along came one of Jack's most memorable roles, as the sailor Billy 'Bad Ass' Buddusky in *The Last Detail*, which had been adapted for the screen by another of Jack's friends, Robert Towne. The director was Hal Ashby. The story concerned two sailors who have to take a 17-year-old recruit from Virginia to New Haven to begin a jail term for theft. En route they decide to give him a last look at life, and the journey turns into five days of swearing, whoring and drinking. As was now becoming the norm with Jack's films, *The Last Detail* was not without its problems. First Chief Justice Warren Burger refused permission for the crew to film Jack drunk on the steps of the Supreme Court in Washington, apparently because Jack had signed a petition for the impeachment of Richard Nixon. The crew was banned from other locations because the film's sentiments upset the Navy. Next, Columbia got nervous about the bad language used and wanted to halve the number of times a certain swear word was used. Towne was furious: 'If it's offensive, it's offensive – what difference does it make if we hear it 40 times or 20?' He won; the film was artistically acclaimed, and Jack earned another Oscar nomination, only to have it snatched from his grasp, this time by Jack Lemmon in *Save The Tiger*.

Off the movie set, Jack had begun what was to be the most enduring relationship of his life. On the back of *The Last Detail* (he could now command $1 million a movie) he was, as usual, hosting parties and flying friends on first-night junkets to Las Vegas to see Sinatra or Bette Midler, or to concerts in New York, or buying ringside seats at sports events, or going on skiing trips to Aspen or Gstaad. Jack had been brooding, though not celibate, since Michelle left, but his eyes lit up when he spotted 22-year-old Anjelica Huston, daughter of

film director John Huston, at one of his parties in Mulholland Drive. She was to stay, on and off, for the next 17 years. She was taken with Jack's eyes: 'And who isn't? They were kind, his whole face lit up when he smiled.' What the roughneck boy from New Jersey saw when he looked at this svelte, sophisticated model who had grown up surrounded by servants and privilege, was 'C-L-A-S-S.' Anjelica's father had directed classics like *The Maltese Falcon*. Coincidentally, many critics likened Jack's screen presence to Bogart's. Her father, too, had an Irish background and had made a career out of womanizing and drinking. There were, Anjelica was to discover – sometimes to her cost – many parallels between her father and Jack Nicholson.

Careerwise, Jack was still making unpredictable decisions. He had turned down the part of Michael Corleone in Francis Ford Coppola's epic, *The Godfather* – although he was tempted by the idea of working with Brando. Instead he accepted the offer of his old friend Robert Evans to star in a movie called *Chinatown*, to be directed by Roman Polanski. Evans wanted his then wife, Ali MacGraw, to co-star, but in the meantime she ran off with Steve McQueen. Jane Fonda turned the part down, and Polanski later chose Faye Dunaway. Jack played dapper private detective J.J. Gittes. Although Jack is most often seen slouching around in jeans and sneakers, he has always professed a love for glamour. This role would dress him in expensive tailoring from head to toe. He based the character on the man he still thought to be his father, John Nicholson, who, before the drink caught hold, had been regarded as something of a dandy at the Easter Parade.

The clothes were the only smooth thing about the movie: the complicated story dealt with corruption in high places, violence, sex, incest and death. And, on set, the sparks flew, particularly between Polanski and Dunaway. Once, when her hair wasn't quite right, Polanski walked up to her, distracting her with small

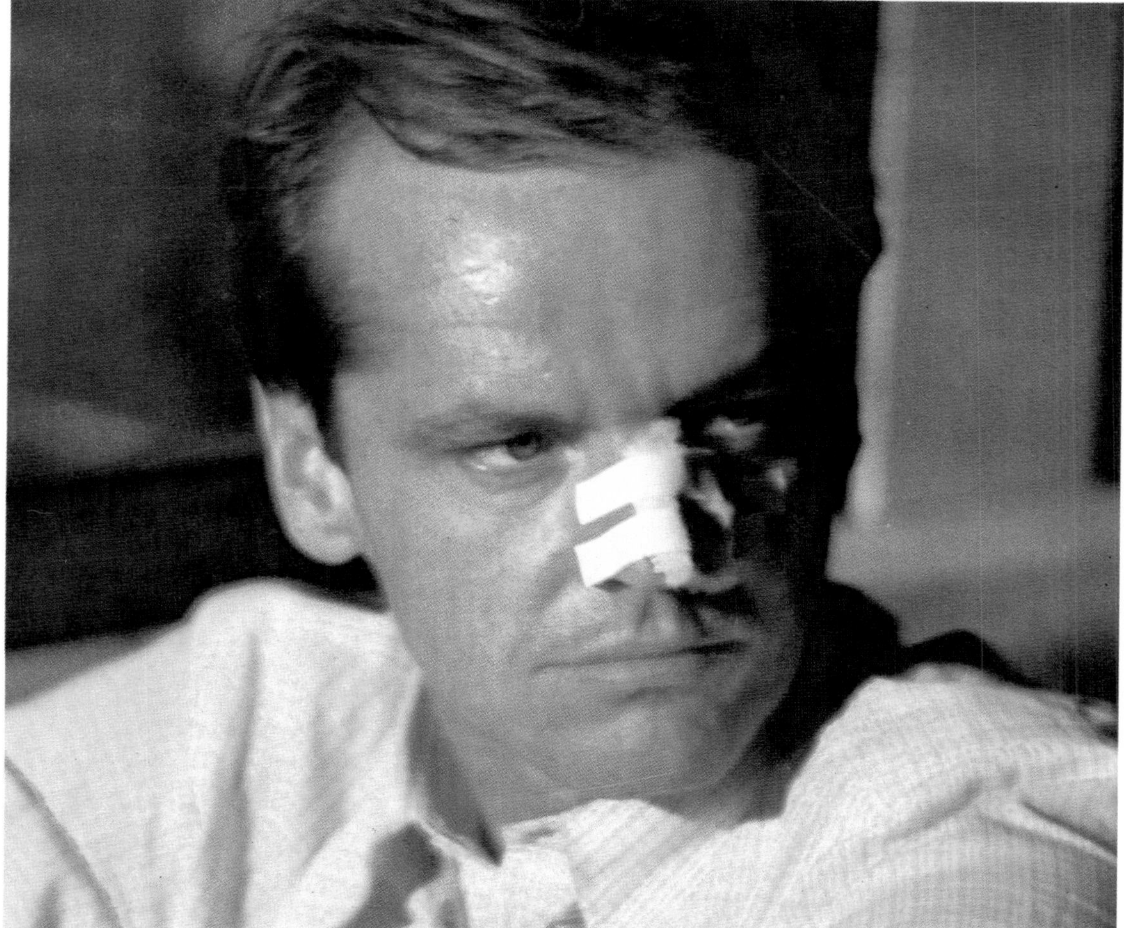

Far left: After a run of flops, Jack landed the role of Billy 'Bad Ass' Buddusky in *The Last Detail.* During shooting there were problems to do with Jack's political beliefs, problems getting the swear words past the censors, and problems with the U.S. Navy. But the critics loved it, and Jack won another Oscar nomination – only to lose out to Jack Lemmon.

Above: Jack arrives at the New York premiere of *The Last Detail* with model Anjelica Huston, daughter of director John Huston. It was to become the most enduring relationship of his life. 'She was C-L-A-S-S,' enthused Jack.

Left: Never a vain actor, Jack appeared throughout most of *Chinatown* wearing a bandage over his nose. The film was directed by Roman Polanski.

Far left, top: Rumors were rife about Jack's supposed real-life affair with Faye Dunaway, his love-interest co-star in *Chinatown*. Although Jack did not deny it, it seems unlikely, given his love for Anjelica. He did console Dunaway, however, who was treated brutally during filming by Polanski.

Far left, bottom: The infamous nose-slitting scene from *Chinatown*. Polanski himself played the thug who injures Jack's character, private detective J.J. Gittes.

Left: Jack was said to have modeled Gittes on the man he still thought to be his father, John Nicholson, the dandy of the Easter Parade. The film confirmed Jack as a major star, but he still didn't win the Oscar.

talk, while pulling the stray hairs from her head. She stormed off and her agent demanded an apology before she would return. Another time she despaired at Polanski's inability to explain what she should be doing: 'But what's my motivation?' 'Motivation? I'll tell you motivation. All the money you're being paid to do it. That's motivation,' barked Polanski. Through all this, Jack tried to act as a mediator, but he fell out with Polanski himself when the director tried to ban him from sneaking off between scenes to catch a basketball game on T.V. featuring his favorite team, the Los Angeles Lakers. *Chinatown* also featured John Huston as the corrupt, incestuous big-businessman and father to Dunaway. At one point he asks Jack's character: 'Are you sleeping with her?' It was more than a little ironic, given Jack's affair with Anjelica.

For all the rows, Jack knew he had a winner in the bag. He had always maintained a friendly competitiveness with Bruce Dern, whom he saw as his only rival, save for Brando. When shooting was complete, he rang Dern to gloat: 'Hey, Dernise, I think you'd better retire. I got it all covered babe, you know what I mean?' The film was indeed an enormous critical and financial success. Jack's performance was singled out by the critics, but he still didn't get the Oscar. Nevertheless, *Chinatown* was the movie that finally confirmed Jack as a major star: no mean feat when you consider that he spent most of the film with a huge bandage over his nose. One reviewer said of his performance: 'Nicholson is the only actor I know who can sneer with charm; he brings a fine, cynical edge to a kind of spruced-up Marlowe.' Jack consequently became the 159th celebrity to be invited to leave his hand- and footprint in the forecourt of the Chinese Theater, and he was also featured on the cover of *Time* magazine.

For all the critical acclaim, Jack still thought of himself as a young actor with a lot to learn. In interviews he played down his success, and said: 'Like most people I just drifted into acting. It was the best goddam piece of drifting I ever did.' Perhaps he knew that the best was yet to come. Besides, he still hadn't won that coveted Oscar . . .

A STAR ARRIVES

Previous pages: A scene from *The Passenger* with actress Maria Schneider. Jack played a T.V. reporter who switches identities with a dead man. Schneider had just created a stir with her steamy role playing opposite Marlon Brando in *Last Tango In Paris*.

Left: Jack only took the role in *The Passenger* because he wanted to work with Michelangelo Antonioni, whose career was in the doldrums after *Zabriskie Point*. Antonioni was famous for the definitive 1960s film, *Blow Up*.

Right: Another ill-fated venture, *The Fortune*, saw Jack teamed with Warren Beatty in a black 'comedy' directed by Mike Nichols.

'I guess this proves there are as many nuts in the Academy as anywhere else' – Jack Nicholson, on receiving his first Oscar for **One Flew Over The Cuckoo's Nest**

It wouldn't be long now before Jack discovered the truth about his family – that his real mother was not Ethel, the woman he had just buried, but June, the woman he believed was his sister and who had died the day he left to film *Ensign Pulver*. For the time being, however, he was none the wiser, and was happy just being with Anjelica and savoring his stardom. He still showed no enthusiasm for safe, mainstream Hollywood productions, and for his next project chose to work with another notoriously difficult director, Michelangelo Antonioni. The Italian director had made it big with the definitive 1960s movie, *Blow Up*, but he had failed to live up to his early promise and had just suffered another critical and box-office failure with the highly indulgent and obscure *Zabriskie Point*. Jack didn't care, however, and even dropped his fee to help Antonioni (the whole project would, in fact, never have been bankrolled unless Jack had come on board), and on signing the contract he announced: 'I am doing this film totally because of Antonioni.' The film, which teamed Jack with Maria Schneider, who was hot from her steamy role with Brando in *Last Tango in Paris*, was called *The Passenger*. In it Jack played a T.V. reporter who is tired of his own life and switches identities with another man who has died. The movie was shot in Europe and Africa.

The press, meanwhile, was having a field day. Rumors of an affair were rife after Faye Dunaway turned up to watch Jack filming in Munich; Anjelica was in

London, and the papers said that he and Dunaway were 'inseparable' after appearing together in *Chinatown*. Whether this was ever true is open to debate, but Jack was in no mood to deny it – after all it was all good publicity. Reporters, and the film's publicists, also tried to drum up stories of an affair between Jack and Schneider and, again, Jack did little to destroy the myth. Later he said: 'Maria has a fantastic screen personality. She is a very challenging actress. We worked beautifully together. She used to say it was because I understood everything that was happening and she understood nothing. She hated the photographers that came round.' Soon there were stories suggesting that Jack was also wooing Anjelica's best friend, Cher. Again, the rumors go to show how lasting the effects of *Carnal Knowledge* had been on his image. Jack was a little disappointed with his relationship with Antonioni, although he happily reported that he had been told that he was the only actor to get on with Antonioni in 25 years. There was little or no direction, but there were plenty of tantrums: 'That's why he's so good,' said Jack. *The Passenger* did little to revive Antonioni's fortunes, but Jack didn't seem to mind.

He flew back to Los Angeles and almost immediately hopped onto an airplane with Anjelica to London, where he had agreed a $50,000 fee for two days' work on a cameo role in Ken Russell's latest venture, a film version of Pete Townsend's rock opera, *Tommy*. Jack played a Harley Street doctor and had to sing, for the first time since his ill-fated duet with Streisand; he joked: 'And let me say I sing better than Oliver Reed in Tommy.' But it was fun, he got to meet Keith Moon, Tina Turner, Elton John – and to be reunited with his *Carnal Knowledge* co-star Ann-Margret.

Previous pages and below: Two further scenes from *The Fortune.* During filming Jack was to learn from *Time* magazine that June was his real mother and Ethel May his grandmother. At his request the story was suppressed by *Time*, only to be splashed all over the pages of the *National Enquirer* in 1980.

While in London the British press fawned over Jack. Female writers purred about his 'rather lovely white teeth' and his sexy 'cobra eyes' – a frequently used phrase coined by Candice Bergen. Jack was giving interviews left, right and center – interviews that tended to concentrate on his now-legendary sex appeal. He denied that he was a chauvinist, yet, when asked the secret of his success, said that 'women love to be frightened.' He said it wasn't just a question of holding a door open for a woman, or noticing what she wears, 'although that does help,' but more 'being able to talk to her, and the basis of conversation with a woman is unbridled curiosity.' He said that the problem with most men, especially younger men, was that they didn't know how to talk to a woman. Jack added that he loved all women, although not always as much as they loved him. One interviewer asked him if he had ever worried about his height (he is, at most, 5ft 10in): 'Oh sure, I'm in a total sweat about it,' drawled Jack. He would not be drawn on the question of marriage to Anjelica, or 'Tootie,' as he had nicknamed her, saying that with one failed marriage behind him he just didn't have 'a policy on it.' But he certainly sounded besotted. He delighted in the fact that Anjelica had quit modeling since being with him, and said that he didn't mind how long he had to wait for her to get ready when they were going out: 'We both love dressing up and going out. I love her in black. She could wear it every day for me. But she is

Below: Despite *The Fortune*'s big-name stars and respected director, this thin 'screwball' comedy, again written by Carol Eastman, was to go down as one of the worst turkeys of Jack's career. One film critic confronted him with the information that no one in the preview audience had laughed. 'I don't believe you,' said a red-faced Jack.

always beautiful.' And then he flew off with her to collect a Best Actor award for *The Last Detail* in Cannes.

Back in Los Angeles, Jack started work on a comedy which teamed him for the first time with Warren Beatty (known as Master B), called *The Fortune*. Mike Nichols ('Big Nick') would direct, and the script had again been written by Carol Eastman.

While filming, Jack got a call from *Time* magazine. They had come across an interesting story about his family: did he know that his real mother was the woman he'd grown up believing was his sister? Jack was shell-shocked. He immediately rang Lorraine, who confirmed the story. Although Jack felt that his world was coming apart at the seams, he quickly composed himself and rang *Time* back, confirming that the story was true, but asking them not to publish it. They agreed, and the public would not come to hear of it until the *National Enquirer* splashed the story all over its front page in 1980. Jack apologized to Nichols for his lack of concentration but, ever the trouper, didn't miss a day's shooting. On release it soon became apparent that the movie was a disaster: at the critics' preview nobody laughed. The public didn't laugh either; but Jack was now a big enough star to brush this failure aside. Besides, he would have the last laugh, because he had just signed up to make *One Flew Over The Cuckoo's Nest*.

The role of Randall Patrick McMurphy, a convicted

These pages: Jack has always had the happy knack of bouncing back from scathing reviews and commercial flops with a real gem of a film, in this case, *One Flew Over The Cuckoo's Nest*. In 1974 he took on the role of Randall Patrick McMurphy, the convicted rapist who convinces his doctors that he is insane in order to avoid a harsh prison sentence, and is instead sent to a psychiatric hospital. In the scene *top left,* McMurphy arrives at the hospital (the film was shot in a real mental hospital in Oregon). *Bottom left,* McMurphy is seen in one of his many confrontations with ward sister Nurse Ratched, played by Louise Fletcher. *Below,* McMurphy is pictured with the other inmates, including a slimmer, more youthful Danny DeVito (front center) and (standing) Will Sampson, the national-park warden who was plucked from obscurity to play Chief.

rapist who convinces doctors he is insane in order to escape a harsh prison sentence, and then stirs up his fellow mental-hospital inmates to rebel against the institution's regime, seemed tailor-made for Jack – and yet it had first been played on stage with limited success by Kirk Douglas. Douglas had snapped up the rights to Ken Kesey's 1962 book before it even hit the book stands. He had tried to interest Hollywood in making it into a movie, but there were no takers. Eventually Douglas had handed over the rights to his actor son, Michael Douglas who, having persuaded respected Czech director Milos Forman to direct the movie, was looking round for a leading man. He thought first of Burt Reynolds – hard to imagine now, but Reynolds was a big box-office draw in 1974. Yet somehow Burt wasn't right . . . and then he thought of Jack Nicholson. This was a strange coincidence, as Jack recalled: 'It's funny. When the book first came out I tried to get an option on the rights and was told they had been bought by Kirk Douglas.'

Two weeks before shooting was due to begin, Jack went to the Oregon State Mental Hospital (the only institution which could be persuaded to allow filming on location) to study the patients. He mixed with them

freely, ate meals with them, and even watched some of them undergoing electric-shock treatment, the procedure which would finally destroy McMurphy. Many of the inmates would actually appear in the film; another pivotal character, Chief, was plucked from his job as a national-park warden to appear: 'Suddenly two men on horses [Jack and Michael Douglas] appeared and offered me a career in movies. I thought they were kidding,' recalled Will Sampson, the Native American who played Chief. The role of Nurse Ratched, the cruel ward sister against whom McMurphy rebels, was turned down by Anne Bancroft, Jane Fonda and Faye Dunaway, before going to Louise Fletcher.

For the 11 weeks of filming Jack rented accommodation for himself and Anjelica. But he was so immersed in the part, so intimidated by the expectations of him in this role of a lifetime, that he was difficult to live with – so much so that Anjelica packed her bags and said she'd see him back in L.A. 'Usually, I don't have much trouble slipping in and out of character but in Oregon I didn't go home from a movie studio, I was going home from a mental institution and there's a certain amount of the character left in you that you can't get rid of; it became harder and harder to create a separation between reality and make-believe because some of the people in there look so normal. You would never know they were murderers,' explained Jack. It was all worth it in the end, of course, because Jack finally won his Best Actor Oscar. In the end the film collected nine nominations and five Oscars, including Best Actress for Louise Fletcher, and Best Director for Milos Forman. No film had been as successful since Claudette Colbert and Clark Gable starred in *It Happened One Night* in 1934. 'I guess this proves there are as many nuts in the Academy as anywhere else,' said a justifiably overjoyed Jack.

Above: Jack plays the clown at the Oscar ceremony following *One Flew Over The Cuckoo's Nest*. From left, producer Saul Zaentz, Louise Fletcher (Best Actress) and Jack (Best Actor). The movie collected nine nominations and five Oscars. No film had been so successful since *It Happened One Night* with Claudette Colbert and Clark Gable.

Right: A delighted Jack holds his much-coveted Oscar aloft – and to think the role of McMurphy had originally been earmarked for Burt Reynolds.

THE SECOND OSCAR

Previous pages: Shelley Duvall as the terrorized wife in *The Shining*, adapted from Stephen King's book and directed by brilliant maverick director, Stanley Kubrick.

Below: Jack and Randy Quaid in a scene from *The Missouri Breaks*. On the back of *One Flew Over The Cuckoo's Nest* Jack earned $1.25 million plus 10% of profits over $12.5 million for just 10 weeks' work for this movie. This helped compensate for having to film in 112°F in the desert in Billings, Montana.

Right: Jack with his lifelong hero, Marlon Brando, in *The Missouri Breaks*. Brando was difficult to work with and later said he didn't think Jack was as good an actor as Robert De Niro.

'I'm sorry I ever said I smoked pot... Besides, it's like womanizing. I'm not sure it ain't good for business' – Jack Nicholson

Jack was on a high after winning the Oscar. He'd been nominated so many times without clinching it that he had been telling friends that he was beginning to think he'd have to die and be awarded one posthumously. It also did no harm whatsoever to his earning capacity: he was offered $1.25 million, plus 10% of profits over $12.5 million, for just 10 weeks' work on a typically 1970s Western called *The Missouri Breaks*. The director was to be Arthur Penn, who had made *Bonnie And Clyde*. But the real attraction for Jack was that it offered the chance to co-star with his lifelong idol, Marlon Brando.

Although Jack and Marlon were neighbors, they hardly knew one another. But, as the Hollywood publicists would have it, Jack leaned over their dividing fence one day and said: 'How d'ya like to make a quick $1 million?' Brando didn't hesitate: he had financial troubles, he was paying out alimony to two ex-wives, a property venture had collapsed, costing him hundreds of thousands of dollars, and he had an expensive new cause, supporting Native Americans. Brando asked for $500,000 a week, but settled for $1 million plus 10% of gross takings over $10 million for five weeks' work. Jack would soon have no illusions about just how difficult Brando could be: problems started almost from the outset, when Brando campaigned for Jack's role to be played instead by a Native American. When filming started, Brando kept himself to himself, and had even

leaned on Penn so that he could get his scenes shot early, while Jack had to hang around in 112°F temperatures in the desert in Billings, Montana.

To aggravate matters further, Brando refused to rehearse with Jack. And while Jack, the consummate movie professional, would turn up on set, line perfect, Brando had to have cue cards all over the place, even pinned to parts of his fellow actors' bodies. 'Why does the greatest actor in the world need cue cards?' Jack asked. 'Because he hasn't learned his lines, that's why,' replied Penn. The 'greatest actor in the world' was also notoriously difficult to direct. Brando would argue every point with Penn. One day he even flounced off set. Jack, as dryly philosophical as ever, said: 'Oh well, another day, another $20,000.' Off set there were complaints from the manager of the nearby War Bonnet Motel that crew members were boozing and womanizing until the early hours; 'They're just a bunch of rednecks,' said Jack.

Afterward Jack felt unsure of the movie's box-office potential. A week before it opened he sold back half of his 10% share of its eventual receipts for $1 million. When payment was not made by the deadline, he filed a suit for breach of contract in the Los Angeles Superior Court. Brando, meanwhile, was less than generous about his co-star, saying: 'Poor old Jack. He was running around cranking the whole thing out while I'm zipping in and out like a firefly. I don't think he's that bright – not as good as Robert De Niro.'

Sticking to his maxim about always wanting to do something different as long as he could afford to, Jack went into an entirely different production, *The Last Tycoon* – ironically with De Niro. The producer was his old friend Sam Spiegel, the director was Elia Kazan,

Far left: Jack and Diane Keaton, who was dating his friend, Warren Beatty (all later to star in *Reds*), visit actor Christopher Lloyd, who played one of the inmates in *One Flew Over The Cuckoo's Nest.*

Left: Jack with Anjelica. His bad behavior and philandering drove Angelica into a well-publicized affair with Ryan O'Neal.

Below: Jack was to keep a low profile during the Roman Polanski underage sex scandal. The offense was alleged to have been committed at Jack's home in Mulholland Drive.

who had made stars of both Brando and James Dean, and the script was written by Britain's Harold Pinter. Spiegel wanted Jack to play the cultured Jewish boy-mogul, Irving J. Thalberg, hero of the novel by F. Scott Fitzgerald; Kazan wanted De Niro. Kazan won, and Jack was offered a cameo as a communist union leader and was paid $150,000. A lot was riding on the film, but it was scathingly received and flopped at the box office. That made two failures in a row, and Jack became desperate to persuade United Artists to let him direct a film called *Moontrap*. They refused to do so unless Jack starred in it too, to which he replied that he couldn't do both well, and the result was stalemate. However, Jack now had other things on his mind, namely the fact that Anjelica was having an affair with one of his best friends, Ryan O'Neal.

Jack's situation was all very familiar to old friends like Don Devlin: 'Jack is such an overwhelming character that girls love him. Then he starts behaving fairly badly, then he starts to love the girl, then he goes chasing after her again, then the relationship changes and the girl gets the upper hand and he becomes like a little boy . . . ' Anjelica took off to London with O'Neal while Jack brooded in Aspen; then he followed her to London. The rift kept the gossip columnists busy all summer – Jack was spotted wining and dining a bevy of beautiful young women, including Jerry Hall; then he and Anjelica patched things up. She next ran off again with O'Neal to Holland, where he was filming *A Bridge Too Far*, while Jack mooned at the paparazzi who swarmed round the yacht in the south of France where he was entertaining various women. Anjelica's jaunt to Holland seemed to prove one humiliation too much for Jack: he literally ordered her back, and, amazingly, she contritely came. Within days they were announcing to the world's press that they were together again, and forever. 'I felt so crummy abandoning him – men like Jack you just don't find anymore,' said Anjelica.

On 24 March 1977 a bombshell landed on Jack, on the day he was due in London to collect his B.A.F.T.A. award as Best Actor for *One Flew Over The Cuckoo's Nest*. Roman Polanski was facing six charges of drugging and raping a 13-year-old girl at Jack's house in Mulholland Drive. Jack was in Aspen at the time, and Roman had tricked the housekeeper into letting him in. Anjelica had arrived home unexpectedly and was unconvinced by Polanski's story that he was working on a photographic commission for a magazine on the beautiful young girls of America. After the arrest police had searched Jack's house and allegedly found a small quantity of cocaine in Anjelica's handbag. She was released on $1500 bail and the charges would later be dropped when she gave evidence against Polanski.

During all this Jack kept a low profile in Aspen. On his return he was fingerprinted to see whether his prints matched those found on a hashish box in the house. They didn't. On the eve of Polanski complying with a 90-day custodial order for psychiatric tests, Jack threw a small dinner party for him. In the event, Polanski only served 48 days before fleeing to France, where he remains in exile, unable to risk working again in the States. Some of the stigma surrounding this sordid case was to stick to Jack Nicholson. When his next film – a comic Western set in Mexico – was released, many reviewers would comment on his 'foggy manner' and his 'peculiar nasal voice.' The implication was that he was stoned on marijuana or cocaine; Jack insisted that he was just trying to sound like Clark Gable. The film, *Goin' South*, was a big break for Mary Steenburgen, an actress Jack literally plucked from obscurity to play a leading role – when she later won an Oscar for Best Supporting Actress in *Melvin And Howard* in 1980, she would say that she owed it all to Jack Nicholson.

However, *Goin' South* was a dismal failure for Jack. What was worse was that the drugs innuendos wouldn't go away. He was later successfully to sue *The Sun* newspaper in London for saying that he had had 'a string of drugs busts' when in fact he had had none. Jack would later say: 'I'm sorry I ever said I smoked pot. I have to put up with being falsely described because it's unhip to bridle at it. Besides, it's like womanizing. I'm not sure it ain't good for business.' Then there would be that smile again, and all was forgiven. Jack still used to tell interviewers that he liked to get high about four times a week, which he thought was 'about average for an American.'

Around this time the *National Enquirer* revealed the truth about Jack's family background, breaking the silence that *Time* magazine had honored when it first got wind of the story back in 1975. Under the headline 'Jack Nicholson's Bizarre Family Secret,' it told the world how Jack had grown up thinking that his mother, June, was his sister, and his grandmother, Ethel May, was his mother. It also carried quotations and a photo-

Far left and left: The cast from *Goin' South*, a comic Western set in Mexico. The film made the leading lady, a hitherto unknown, Mary Steenburgen, a star, but its failure could have broken Jack.

Below left: When *Goin' South* was released many critics commented on Jack's 'foggy manner' and 'peculiar nasal voice' – implying that he was stoned on marijuana or cocaine. Jack angrily denied this and said that he regretted ever admitting getting high about four times a week, which he considered 'about average for an American.'

graph of Don Furcillo Rose, Jack's real father, who claimed he had been very much in love with June and that, on learning she was pregnant, he had married her in a secret service in Maryland where couples can wed with 'no questions asked.' On their return to Neptune, he said, Ethel May, who didn't know of their marriage, told him never to see June again because he was older, divorced and, anyway, she had great hopes of her beautiful daughter making it in Hollywood. Following this story, Don, now in his seventies and going blind, told other reporters that his wife, Dorothy, had written to Jack, begging him to acknowledge Don, as long ago as 1973. Jack had eventually rung one day and said: 'This is Jack Nicholson, I hear you're family.' He had asked if there was anything they needed and they had maintained occasional telephone contact for a few years. Don said his dearest wish was to see his son before he died and noted how, ironically, it was he, and not June or Ethel May, who had lived to see Jack win an Oscar.

Jack maintained a dignified silence when the story broke, but he admitted to having been 'stunned' by the revelations. Meanwhile, however, he had his career to think of. With three disasters in the can, Jack badly needed a hit. It came in the form of a horror movie, based on a Stephen King book, and directed by Stanley Kubrick, called *The Shining*. Kubrick had wanted to work with Jack ever since *Easy Rider*. He had hoped

Right: Jack with his screen son in Stanley Kubrick's *The Shining*. The film took 18 months to shoot on location in London because of Kubrick's legendary perfectionism. 'Just because you're a perfectionist doesn't mean you're perfect,' quipped Jack.

Below: Jack's character, writer Jack Torrance, descends into madness while working as a caretaker during the summer at a seasonal hotel. Off-camera, however, he was living it up in Chelsea, London.

Far right: The infamous scene in which Jack Torrance is trying to murder his wife, played by Shelley Duvall. The 'Heeeeere's Johnny' line was Jack's own – a chilling spoof on the introduction to America's *Tonight* show with Johnny Carson.

These pages: Jack had been interested in filming a remake of *The Postman Always Rings Twice* ever since the days when there had been talk of him starring in it with one-time lover Michelle Phillips. His eventual co-star was Jessica Lange, who played Cora, the frustrated wife of a brutish husband who is murdered by her lover, played by Jack. For all its raunchiness, and its pedigree production team – director Bob Rafelson, scriptwriter David Mamet – the film was not a critical or commercial success in the States.

Following pages, top left: Jack looking every inch the established movie star. *Right:* Jack's next project was *Reds*, written and directed by Warren Beatty, who starred as John Reed, the all-American boy who became a communist and lived in Moscow, writing a bestseller, *Ten Days That Shook The World*. The movie starred Beatty's real-life lover Diane Keaton. Jack played alcoholic playwright Eugene O'Neill.

Jack would play Napoleon for him, but could never get the backing. Now he was offering him the role of aspiring writer, Jack Torrance, who takes a summer job as a caretaker in a deserted and haunted seasonal hotel, and descends into madness, threatening to kill his wife, played by Shelley Duvall. The film would take Jack to London for about 18 months, and would prove to be one of the most arduous roles of his career so far. Kubrick was famous for his constant retakes and punishing schedules; 'Just because you're a perfectionist doesn't mean you're perfect,' griped Jack. The producers paid him $1.25 million, plus his usual percentage, and rented him an expensive mansion in Chelsea's Cheyne Walk, also providing the use of a Daimler and the services of a chauffeur called George.

Away from the set Jack was working late, then going to parties and clubs with a host of girlfriends in London. Margaret Trudeau, the ex-wife of former Canadian prime minister Pierre Trudeau, claimed that she filled in Jack's off-screen moments, driving around London behind the inscrutable George and discovering 'just how much room there is in the back of a Daimler.' Jack denied this, and thus placated Anjelica. However, he was also photographed out on the town with 23-year-old Marilyn Monroe lookalike, actress Linda Kerridge.

The Shining was not well received by the critics; Jack was accused of going over the top, but the movie nevertheless made a mint and became one of the highest-grossing films ever for Warner Brothers. The most famous line in *The Shining* was nearly never shown. When Torrance axes his way through the bathroom door to terrorize his wife, he calls: 'Heeeeere's Johnny.' The line was Jack's, but it was temporarily lost on Kubrick, who was unfamiliar with the introduction to America's *Tonight* show, with Johnny Carson.

For his next project, Jack resurrected the idea of a remake of *The Postman Always Rings Twice*, with old friend Bob Rafelson as director, world-famous cinematographer Steve Nykist (renowned for his work with Ingmar Bergman), and a script by David Mamet. Jack would play the John Garfield role as the aimless ex-con who gets involved in a steamy affair and murder, and Jessica Lange would play the Lana Turner role of Cora. Jack was interested in playing up the sex, and the kitchen-table scene was to become one of his most memorable. For all the raunchiness and the brilliant script, the movie was not successful in the States,

although it was more popular in Europe.

By now Jack had undertaken the role of alcoholic writer Eugene O'Neill in Warren Beatty's grandiose pet project, *Reds*, also starring Beatty's current love, Diane Keaton, plus respected veterans Maureen Stapleton and Gene Hackman. The film centered on John Reed, an all-American boy who became a radical communist, and was present in Moscow to witness Lenin's rise to power (he remains the only American to be buried in the Kremlin). His book, *Ten Days That Shook The World*, had been a constant fascination to Beatty. With its massive budget – some estimates say $30 million, some $50 million, and Jack's fee alone was $3 million – *Reds* was one of the most talked-about movies since *Cleopatra*. Making his directorial debut, Beatty was –

CANADIAN BANK
1931
GREYHOUND
LINES

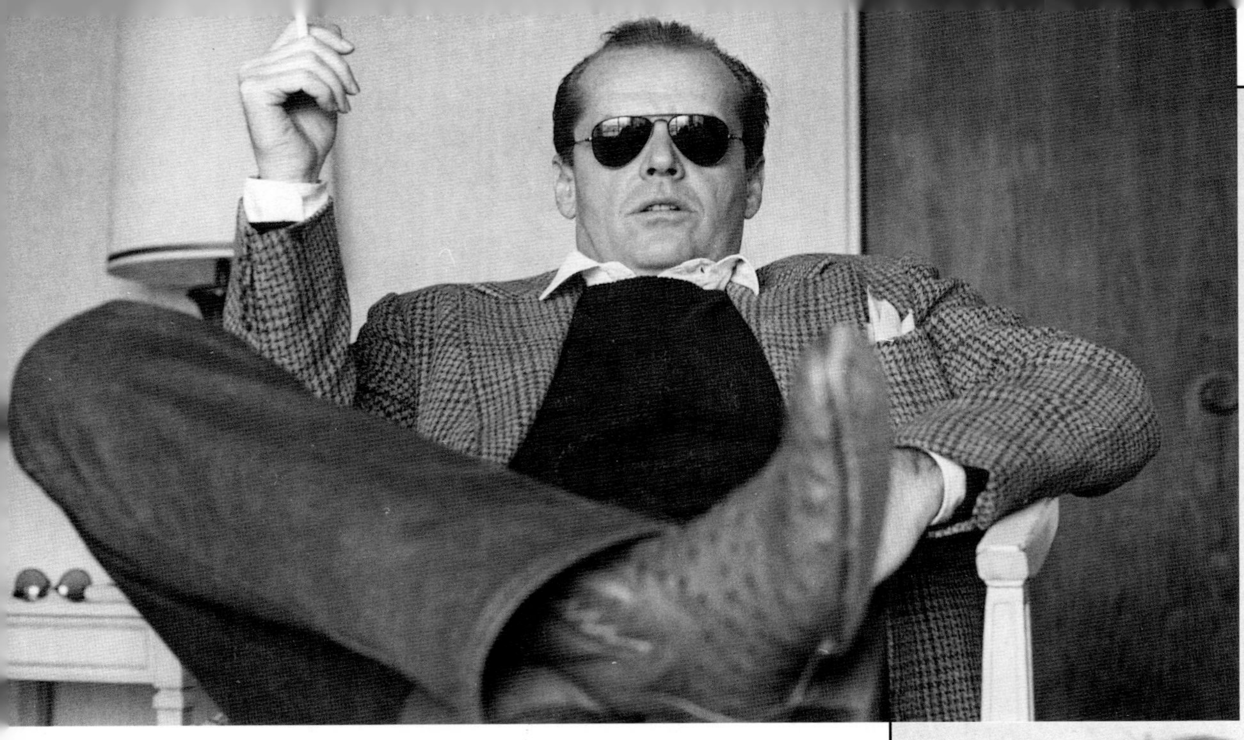

not surprisingly – unsure of himself. He would demand 20 or 30 retakes and, by the end, had 130 hours of film to edit down into 3 hours and 19 minutes.

There were rumors that Jack had a huge crush on Keaton and, at one point, when O'Neill hands her character a poem, it was alleged that it was one which Jack had written for Keaton. He played along with this gossip good-humoredly – after all he was always happy to hype his films. The film won him a Best Supporting Actor nomination at the Oscars, but the best tribute of all was to come from O'Neill's daughter, Oona. She wrote to him: 'After a lifetime's acquired indifference I fell in love with my father, thanks to you.' 'It was the greatest compliment I've had,' commented Jack.

After *Reds* came *The Border*, again for a friend, this time the British director Tony Richardson. Jack played Charlie Smith, a patrolman stopping illegal immigrants crossing from Mexico into Texas. Jack was suffering almost constant back pain after an injury he had sustained while in London for *The Shining*, but he still managed to turn in a creditable performance. Overall, however, the movie was felt to be too bleak, and out of step with the new wave of youth-market movies that were to become the norm during the 1980s. Indeed, Jack was still playing anti-heroes when heroes were becoming more fashionable in Spielberg films such as *Star Wars, ET* and *Jaws*.

By 1982 Jack had been working almost solidly all year and needed time off to reflect on what to do next. His hair was receding, his waistline was expanding, and he was 44. Despite good reviews for *The Border*, he was experiencing a crisis of confidence; he needed a very different vehicle to stay on top. He decided to take the next year off to mull it over, and was seen dining Princess Caroline of Monaco, Rachel Ward, and Petula Clark's 17-year-old daughter, Cathy Wolff.

Little could he have known that the role that was to establish his change of direction was just around the corner, or that he might owe his successful transition to, of all people, Burt Reynolds . . .

THE POWER PLAYER

Below: Jack as middle-aged, paunchy, former astronaut Garry Breedlove in *Terms of Endearment* – a lovable rogue.

'I've chased girls all my life. By nature I'm not monogamous, but it doesn't make any difference because women suspect you whether you are or not' – Jack Nicholson

When director James L. Brooks was looking around for a male actor to take the role of a middle-aged retired astronaut who manages to seduce brittle widow Aurora Greenway out of 15 years of celibacy, he might not immediately have thought of Jack Nicholson. *Terms of Endearment*, while it would deal with tragedy, was essentially a rather frothy concoction, and a vehicle for the over-the-top acting abilities of Shirley MacLaine and the equally feisty Debra Winger. Several leading men were considered. Burt Reynolds, on paper an obvious choice and still a box-office winner at the time, turned it down. So where were they going to find somebody who could be a slob, paunchy and yet still believably sexy and engaging? Suddenly Brooks wondered why it hadn't occurred to him before – Jack Nicholson.

Brooks put in a call and sent a script round right away. Jack accepted instantly, saying: 'How many scripts make you cry?' In truth, he knew it was just the kind of role he needed to broaden his image. And there was always the fee: $1.25 million, plus profits. At the end of the day *Terms of Endearment* was said to have earned him $7 million. But the main attraction was that the role of Gary Breedlove gave him the opportunity to play a lovable rogue, something he knew he could do in his sleep. The role called on him to display an unflattering bulging waistline: 'That's O.K., I'll just swell it out, I call it my baby-elephant belly,' he assured Brooks. Besides, he had never been a slave to vanity; he had always refused make-up and never insisted on special lighting as did so many other film stars. And, after all, how many romantic leading men would agree to play almost an entire movie with a sticking plaster over their nose, as Jack had in *Chinatown?*

Terms of Endearment was a runaway success, gaining 11 Academy Award nominations and winning five: Best Picture, Best Director, Best Adapted Screenplay, Best Actress for MacLaine, and Best Supporting Actor for Jack. In typically laid-back style he sauntered to the podium at the Oscars ceremony, raised a fist and said in a nonchalant drawl: 'All you rock people down at the Roxy and up in the Rockies, rock on!' Nobody knew

what he meant, but it didn't matter – Jack had achieved a double in the Academy's history; only two other actors had done it – Robert De Niro and Jack Lemmon.

Jack enjoyed working with MacLaine, he said she was 'a kind of question-asking machine,' and, of course, he had known her socially for years through his friendship with her brother, Warren Beatty. She was more forthright: 'I have wanted to work with Jack Nicholson since his chicken-salad scene in *Five Easy Pieces* – and to have him in bed with me was such middle-aged joy,' she told the Academy.

Meanwhile, Jack had committed himself to making *Prizzi's Honor*, a black comedy about an inept Mafia hitman, Charley Partanna, which was to be directed by John Huston and would co-star Anjelica and Kathleen Turner. No matter how hard he tried, Jack apparently could not understand his character, and is reputed to have only taken the part for Anjelica's sake. As with all his projects, however, he threw himself into it body and soul, reading about the Mafia, studying hard to get the Brooklyn accent right, saying everything with a stiff

Previous pages: After *Heartburn*, Jack teamed up for the second time with Meryl Streep in *Ironweed*, a bleak 'message' film about street people, directed by *Kiss Of The Spider Woman* director Hector Babenco.

Above: Jack with Shirley MacLaine, who played brittle widow Aurora Greenway. *Terms of Endearment* was said to have earned Jack $7 million, plus an Oscar for Best Supporting Actor.

Left: Jack at the 1984 Oscar ceremony with, from left, Best Actor Robert Duvall, Best Actress Shirley MacLaine, and Best Supporting Actress Linda Hunt.

upper lip, and even going on expeditions to buy Charley's strange wardrobe from secondhand shops in Los Angeles.

During filming he and Anjelica stayed in separate hotels; she was soon to buy her own bungalow just round the corner from Mulholland Drive, but both insisted that all was well with their relationship. It certainly seems as if it was, because, though he would hardly have sniffed at the $3.6 million fee (his price more than doubled after *Terms of Endearment*), there can be little doubt that he took the role to help Anjelica's career and, indeed, she won an Oscar for Best Supporting Actress. The critics, however, were divided about the movie. One described *Prizzi's Honor* as '*The Godfather* played by The Munsters.'

Behind the scenes Jack was desperately trying to drum up financial backing for a film that was to become an obsession with him: the sequel to *Chinatown, The Two Jakes*. He had formed a production company with *Chinatown*'s original scriptwriter Robert Towne, and with Robert Evans, who was to produce the movie and play the second Jake. They intended to make the movie themselves, take no fee, and simply reap the rewards of the profits they were certain it would make. In reality the battle to get the film onto the screen would take many traumatic twists and turns before its even-

Far left, top: Jack with, from left, Kathleen Turner, John Huston and Anjelica in *Prizzi's Honor*, a black comedy about the Mafia, directed by Huston. One critic described it as '*The Godfather* played by The Munsters.' Jack never understood his character, and is reported to have taken the part only to please Angelica.

Far left, bottom: Jack cheers on his favorite basketball team, the L.A. Lakers.

Left: Jack in *Heartburn*, his first collaboration with Meryl Streep. The movie was written by Nora Ephron, and was based on her real-life break-up with husband and Watergate journalist Carl Bernstein. The director was Mike Nichols.

tual release five years later in 1990.

Jack's next film was *Heartburn*. He was given the script by director Mike Nichols only three days before filming was due to begin, and arrived on set without even knowing his character's name. But he couldn't resist the opportunity of playing opposite the greatest movie actress of her generation, Meryl Streep.

Heartburn, adapted for the screen by Nora Ephron, was based on her best-selling book, which was a thinly-veiled account of her husband and ex-Watergate journalist Carl Bernstein's affair with Margaret Jay, then wife of the British ambassador to America, Peter Jay. Unusually, Bernstein's lawyers had managed to negotiate script approval and, as a result, Jack was instructed not to play Carl, but to invent a character with considerably more charm. Many said Jack simply played himself – a few leers here, a raised eyebrow there, and $3.6 million more in his bank account. Easy.

Rumors began to abound that Jack had fallen in love with Streep. Gossip columnists started to talk about their 'sexual chemistry,' and some stories alleged that Anjelica had stormed out in a rage when he put up a life-sized poster of Streep in the living room of his home in Mulholland Drive. Always one to keep an eye on publicity, Jack did little to play down the early stories. Enigmatically, he told interviewers: 'Meryl is my idol. She was so good; I was all at sea, floundering around, but I could see that we would be fine because she was doing great. You do fall in love with . . . with . . . certain, um . . . creative situations . . .' One can only wonder what repercussions Streep suffered from Jack's little games with the press, back home with her sculptor husband, Don Gummer.

The film had a mixed reception and didn't make much money; most reviewers felt it lacked bite and believability once the film-makers had watered down the vitriol of Ephron's attack on Bernstein.

From *Heartburn* Jack went home to Anjelica, and then on one of his regular solo jaunts to Aspen. It was there, in February 1986, that he met British model and aspiring actress Karen Mayo-Chandler. She would later claim that he suggested that she and a female friend join him in bed; she refused and was snubbed by him the next time they met at a night club in Los Angeles. He then apologized to her when they met again at a charity dinner, and later took her to dinner at Robert Evans' and on to watch a movie at Warren Beatty's. It was then, she alleged, that their steamy affair began. For the time being, Jack was having his cake and eating it – still telling journalists how much he adored Anjelica, or 'Angel,' and how often he proposed to her, while fooling around with the nubile Miss Mayo-

Left: Jack and Anjelica had stayed together through countless traumas. He was thrilled when her acting talents were recognized with a Best Supporting Actress Oscar for *Prizzi's Honor.*

Above: Many thought Jack was ideal to play 'horny little devil,' Darryl van Horne in *The Witches Of Eastwick.* He starred with, from left, Cher, Susan Sarandon and Michelle Pfeiffer.

Chandler. In the end, however, this indiscretion was to be the last straw for the long-suffering Anjelica.

It was almost as if Jack was in training for his next role as Darryl van Horne, in George Miller's *The Witches Of Eastwick*, based on a book by John Updike. Jack was paid $5 million for the movie and relished every moment of it. Feminists were up in arms again as van Horne seduced three women in turn, played by Cher, Michelle Pfeiffer and Susan Sarandon. The film also gave Jack the excuse to talk to journalists about sex. 'I've been studying to play the devil,' he announced, 'of course, a lot of people think I've been preparing for it all my life!' Warming to his subject, he said that he didn't know why women found him so attractive, it was just that he seemed to have something that was 'invisible but unfailing.' And, he added: 'I've chased girls all my life. By nature I'm not monogamous, but it doesn't make any difference because women suspect you whether you are or not. Sex is my favorite subject but it's scary for me to talk about it because of Anjelica.'

The Witches Of Eastwick was a huge commercial success, eventually taking $125 million, with a respectable percentage of that going to Jack. He then picked up another $5 million for *Ironweed*, again starring Meryl Streep. By now Jack was becoming worried about his ballooning weight, and demanded that the producers rent him a house with a pool so that he could exercise each day. He also insisted on a $70,000-a-day penalty clause if shooting ran over 69 days. Meanwhile, Streep, who is happily married, was becoming irritated by his tendency to hint at an off-screen romance. As with Diane Keaton after *Reds*, Jack felt obliged to set the record straight, saying: 'How does anybody know what I feel for Meryl? I am not in love with her and Meryl is not in love with me. She's a happily married woman who is dedicated to her husband and kids.' Even this unequivocal statement did little to dampen the enthusiasm of gossip columnists who were likening the two to a modern-day Spencer Tracy and Katharine Hepburn.

Ironweed, about an alcoholic down-and-out, Francis Phelan [Jack], and his relationship with Helen, a one-time concert pianist who has become a bag lady [Streep], was a bleak, intelligent 'message' film, directed by Hector Babenco, who had made his name with *Kiss Of The Spider Woman*. It was critically well received, and both stars were nominated for Oscars. But the movie struggled to make money in a climate where the biggest-grossing films were *Ghostbusters,*

Below left and right: Jack pictured in two scenes from *The Witches of Eastwick. Left* as the wealthy newcomer who seduces Cher, Sarandon and Pfeiffer and, *right*, after he has been unmasked as the devil.

The film angered feminists, who objected to the one-dimensional portrayal of women, and it was generally not considered a worthy adaptation of the book by John Updike.

Right: Jack as down-and-out Francis Phelan in *Ironweed.* He was widely rumored to have fallen in love with co-star Meryl Streep and, said the gossip columnists, Anjelica had demanded that he remove a life-sized portrait of Streep from the wall of his home in Mulholland Drive.

Gremlins, Superman, Beverly Hills Cop and *Back To The Future.*

Between projects, Jack next agreed to do a quick, unbilled cameo as a villainous T.V.-station executive for James Brooks, in *Broadcast News.* During all this activity Anjelica had been in Ireland, working on her dying father's last film, *The Dead.* Things had been strained between her and Jack of late and this, together with her prolonged absence, sent him scurrying back into the arms of Karen Mayo-Chandler. Outwardly, however, he was still talking as if he and Anjelica were the model of togetherness, and it was widely reported that he had promised to honor John Huston's dying wish that he should marry Anjelica. Later, and to devas-

tating effect, Mayo-Chandler would claim that on the eve of Huston's funeral Jack and she had enjoyed a passionate night together. 'I had to ask myself,' she confided, 'why he wasn't consoling Anjelica.'

For the time being, however, Jack's cover with regard to his love life was safe. On the career front, the wheels were being set in motion for a major new project. While working on *The Witches Of Eastwick,* Jack had met up with up-and-coming producers Peter Guber and Jon Peters. They had approached him about the possibility of playing the Joker in a film version of the comic-strip hero, Batman. 'Babe, you've got to be joking,' sneered Jack, 'I wouldn't do that even if Warner Brothers paid me $50 million!' The thing is, they did, and Jack, never one to resist temptation, would soon become the highest-paid actor in the history of Hollywood.

WMGM

HOLLYWOOD'S FAVORITE MAVERICK

Previous pages: Jack Nicholson and Warren Beatty – the two self-styled superstuds of Hollywood – enjoying themselves at the Mike Tyson-Leon Spinks heavyweight title bout in 1988.

Below: Jack was first approached to play the Joker in *Batman* by up-and-coming producers Peter Guber and Jon Peters while he was filming *The Witches Of Eastwick*; he turned their initial advances down flat.

Right: Jack in a memorably Gothic scene from *Batman*. The multimillion-dollar Gotham City set was constructed at Pinewood Studios, just outside London.

'Better pass boldly into that other world in the full glory of some passion than fade and wither dismally with age' – Jack Nicholson's favorite quotation from* The Dubliners*, by James Joyce

Candice Bergen once said that all Jack's friends call him "The Weaver," because he weaves such magical stories.' Magic was perhaps the only thing that could save him in the next couple of years when all his 'chicks' would come home to roost, and he would finally lose the 'love of my life,' Anjelica.

He would also, of course, become rich beyond his wildest dreams. Guber and Peters weren't about to be put off that easily. Having been given the go-ahead by Warner Brothers to make Jack an offer he couldn't refuse to play the Joker, they began to woo him relentlessly, first bringing young director Tim Burton to visit him in Aspen, and then flying him on an all-expenses-paid trip to London to see the multimillion-dollar Gotham City set they were constructing at Pinewood Studios, just outside London.

In London he lived it up as usual, and was photographed out on the town with 22-year-old glamour model, Charlotte Weston. Back in L.A. his affair with Karen Mayo-Chandler was over, and she was said to be touting her story around the press. She would, said her agent, 'sing like a bird' for $150,000. Jack had always admitted that he was intolerant of failings in others, but considered his own failings 'rather charming and cute.' So when he thought Karen was trying to negotiate for 'hush' money, he told her bluntly: 'You must do what you have to do.' Perhaps he simply

thought that a young woman with an eye on a film career wouldn't dare tangle with the biggest star in Tinseltown, or perhaps he had underestimated the impact of his latest indiscretion on Anjelica. A month or so later Jack went to the fashionable Hollywood night club, Helena's, where he was introduced to 26-year-old waitress and aspiring actress, Rebecca Broussard. She had been married, but was now separated from Warners' record producer Richard Perry. Who knows what transpired between them that night but, within months, the *National Enquirer* was on the scent of a big story when it casually mentioned that she had been spotted driving Jack's black Range Rover in Aspen.

Jack, by now, was getting more interested in *Batman*. His initial reservations about rookie director Burton and actor Michael Keaton as Batman were fading; so much so that he fought for his role to be beefed up so that he was filming for 100 days, rather than the mere 21 at first envisaged. Furthermore, the producers had come up with a $6 million basic fee, plus percentages on profits, record royalties and merchandising.

In the event, Jack's knack for over-the-top performances reached a zenith in *Batman* – he simply camped Keaton off the screen. The critics were thrilled, and the almost unprecedented hype brought the crowds flocking in. *Batman* took $250 million in its first four weeks in America alone, and Jack's eventual cut was to be somewhere in the region of $60 million. He was, he said, 'extremely financially viable' but, when asked if he would be doing a sequel, snarled: 'The Joker's dead. Didn't you see the movie?' Indeed, when the sequel became a reality, Jack was telling everyone that he'd had enough of the *Batman* hoopla, that money wasn't everything, and that he wanted to undertake work that was more appealing to him creatively.

He was referring, of course, to *The Two Jakes*, the film he had been obsessively trying to make for over five years. He finally began work on it in early 1989. From the outset his 'baby,' which would follow the fortunes of private detective J.J. Gittes 11 years on, had been dogged with disasters. Of the trio that had originally set out to make it, only Jack was left. Robert Towne, the scriptwriter, had been concerned about Robert Evans' ability to produce and act in it; a rather messy showdown had ensued that was to damage irreparably the two men's friendship. Then Evans – once the golden

These pages: Pictured here are more thrilling scenes from *Batman*, including, *above,* the pivotal confrontation scene with Michael Keaton. Jack is believed to have made $60 million from the movie, but refused to make a sequel. 'The Joker's dead. Didn't you see the movie?' he growled when cornered by the press.

boy of Paramount – had been linked, albeit vaguely, to a murder enquiry which led back to drugs barons in Colombia. Jack was desperate to find a director and approached Polanski, Bernardo Bertolucci and, before his death, John Huston; all three were unavailable. Eventually he decided to direct it himself. He explained: 'The movie wouldn't have been made if I hadn't directed it. That's the main reason I did it. Period.'

Jack began filming with a fairly modest $19-million budget, and had wrapped the movie up by the summer of 1989. It was originally scheduled for release that Christmas but, because of Jack's indecision in editing it (which was, no doubt, intensified by the difficulties which were looming in his personal life), it was put back, first to May 1990, then to Christmas 1990.

In October that year Karen Mayo-Chandler finally sold her story to *Playboy* magazine, and soon became a much sought-after guest on T.V. chat shows across America. Jack was mortified. In all his years of philandering, he had never before suffered this kind of humiliation. This was a no-blushes-spared account of their nights together – 'I don't mind admitting that I learned everything I know about sex from Jack,' cooed Karen. She was indeed singing like a bird about his sexual prowess and stamina, revealing that Jack was a 'non-stop sex machine' but, more embarrassingly, she claimed that he would chase her around the bedroom wearing nothing but blue silk shorts and socks, that he kept his strength up with a pile of peanut butter and jelly sandwiches, that he liked to spank her and take kinky pictures with a Polaroid camera, and so on. The man who had built a reputation on his success with women was left cringing.

Anjelica, who had known something of the story, was livid. But the worst was yet to come . . . just a few months later gossip columnists were telling the world that Rebecca Broussard was pregnant – by Jack. This was the final humiliation for Anjelica, who had always privately hoped that she would have Jack's children. She drove straight to Paramount Studios, where he

These pages, above and left: Jack had been trying to make *The Two Jakes*, the sequel to *Chinatown*, for five years. The film was dogged with production difficulties and, in the end, Jack had to step in to direct the movie himself, as well as having to recreate the character of J.J. Gittes. He told reporters: 'The movie wouldn't have been made if I hadn't directed it. That's the main reason I did it. Period.' Meanwhile, off screen, *left*, Jack was seriously embarrassed by the kiss-and-tell revelations of Karen Mayo-Chandler in October 1989. 'I don't mind admitting that I learned everything I know about sex from Jack,' cooed Karen.

Above: Just months after the Karen Mayo-Chandler scandal, Anjelica finally left Jack after he confirmed that Rebecca Broussard, a 26-year-old waitress, was pregnant with his child. Here the parents-to-be are seen leaving Chasen's Restaurant in Beverly Hills.

Right: Jack pictured with Diana Ross, a platonic friend, at the 33rd Grammy Awards.

Far right: Rebecca and Jack's daughter, Lorraine, at L.A.'s Children's Museum with Shelley Duvall, who co-starred with Jack in *The Shining*.

was editing *The Two Jakes*, and demanded: 'Is this true?' He had little choice but to admit it. Slapping him hard across the face, Anjelica stormed out, vowing: 'This is it. Enough is enough. We're finished.' Jack immediately moved Rebecca to Aspen to get her away from the press.

By Christmas the ice between him and Anjelica had started to thaw. She said: 'Jack Nicholson has given me the worst two yuletide presents I have ever received in my life,' but added, 'he is a soul mate and I hate to think of a world without him. It would be dismal.' Meanwhile he was telling reporters that he didn't feel guilty for falling in love with Rebecca, but that Anjelica had a 'legitimate grievance' and 'some people will think I treated her very badly.' He went on: 'I would not expect Miss Huston to react in any other way than the way she did. I consider her impeccable – always have, always will.'

Left: Jack chats with a basketball player at a L.A. Lakers game. He has been a devoted fan of the sport since his school days, and once had a serious row with Roman Polanski when he wanted to catch a game on television during the filming of *Chinatown*.

Below: Jack pictured with his daughter Lorraine at another L.A. Lakers game. Whatever his shortcomings, he has always loved his children. He maintained a good relationship with Jennifer, the child from his marriage to Sandra Knight, and is nowadays besotted with Lorraine, whom he calls 'Liddy Poo.' Lorraine also has a younger brother, Raymond.

His daughter, Jennifer, rallied to his defense, saying that her father was her best friend, and that she had long been a friend of Rebecca's. When newsmen pointed to the fact that Rebecca was the same age as Jennifer, Jack, in his characteristically raffish way, replied: 'Girls in their early twenties know not to trust their girl friends around their fathers.' He still appeared to have 'no policy' on marriage, however, and instead bought Rebecca a separate $1.5 million mansion in the nearby San Fernando Valley.

On 16 April 1990 Rebecca gave birth to a baby girl, Lorraine, named after Jack's aunt. Jack attended the birth. He said: 'She opened her eyes and seemed to look me over. It took maybe 10 seconds, but in that time I knew I had to protect her for the rest of my life.' Whether this sealed it for Anjelica is hard to tell, but just three months later she married controversial pony-tailed sculptor Robert Graham.

Later that year, when *The Two Jakes* (featuring a small role for Rebecca) was finally released, it was dismissed by the critics as self-indulgent and bleak. It had been Jack's third attempt at directing, but it had not been lucky. He was morose, but tried to make the best of it, saying that he thought the movie would come to be regarded as a minor classic of its genre and adding: 'I always said it would be presumptuous of me to believe I could direct *The Two Jakes* as well as Roman did *Chinatown*.'

These pages: Even a star of Jack Nicholson's stature can make mistakes and, throughout his erratic career, he has made more than a few. A prime example came in 1991, when he filmed *Man Trouble* with Ellen Barkin.

Sporting a new mustache, he played seedy dog trainer Harry Bliss who falls in love, against all the odds, with opera singer Joan Spruance. The critics hated the movie, calling it 'a dog of a film' when it was released in 1992.

Although preoccupied with fatherhood at 53, Jack now committed himself to undertaking three new movies. The first was *Man Trouble*, billed as a romantic thriller, co-starring Ellen Barkin, and directed and scripted by Bob Rafelson and Carol Eastman respectively. Jack played down-at-heel dog trainer Harry Bliss who comes to the rescue of opera singer Joan Spruance [Barkin] when a mysterious intruder breaks into her apartment; against all the odds, they fall in love. Jack pocketed another $5 million for this, but the critics were savage, calling it 'a dog of a film' when it was released in 1992.

Jack's next part was a supporting role in the blockbusting 'brat pack' movie, *A Few Good Men*. It was directed by Rob Reiner (of *When Harry Met Sally* fame) and scripted by David Mamet. Jack was paid $5 million for 10 days' work as the tough, unscrupulous marine colonel Nathan Jessup in a courtroom drama which also starred Tom Cruise, Demi Moore and Kiefer Sutherland. Jack confided to Reiner: 'The biggest difficulty was walking into the first rehearsal and everyone scurrying to their seats when the old guy came in. I felt like the Lincoln Memorial.' His performance was electric, and he was widely tipped, although wrongly, to win a second Best Supporting Actor Oscar.

Just before filming started, Jack had taken a holiday with Rebecca and 'Liddy Poo,' as he called his daughter, in the south of France. The couple gladly posed for the paparazzi and, roughly nine months later, would have another child, Raymond. It was a portrait of family happiness, and they appeared to have shrugged off yet another kiss-and-tell story, this time from former porn star, Serina Robinson, aged 28, who claimed to have been Jack's occasional lover for the past year while she was also dating his *Batman* co-star Michael Keaton.

Jack's performance in *Hoffa*, his next project, would become widely acknowledged as his greatest since *One Flew Over The Cuckoo's Nest*. It was directed by one of his co-stars from that movie, Danny DeVito, and told the life story of the hard-nosed American Teamsters union boss, who challenged the U.S. establishment at the highest level; was rumored to have Mafia connections which implicated him in the shooting of Robert Kennedy; was jailed in 1964 for jury-tampering

LICE LINE
PO

These pages, far left: Jack plays the movie star to the hilt at a charity premiere of *A Few Good Men. Left*, Jack pictured in a scene from the film with Tom Cruise. The cast also included Demi Moore and Kiefer Sutherland. *Below*, Jack was electric as the much-decorated, but unscrupulous marine colonel Nathan Jessup, but felt as old as the Lincoln Memorial in comparison with the young cast.

and fraud; and was finally thought to have been murdered by the Mafia when he vanished without trace in 1975.

For $6 million, plus a percentage of the profits, Jack had to sit in make-up for three hours before each day's shooting, as plastic implants were put into his cheeks, putty was used to thicken his nose, his chin and stomach were padded out, and his sideburns were cut short. He also, according to DeVito, spent literally hours watching newsreels of Jimmy Hoffa to perfect his gait, his mannerisms and his harsh, high-pitched Mid-western twang. 'I didn't just act Jimmy Hoffa, I became him. Like me, he had his faults, but from the second I started studying him I knew here was a guy after my own heart. I love his color, his flashiness, his egotism,' said Jack.

In August 1992, as *Hoffa* was coming up for release, Jack was talking to the press again, only this time about the vexed question of his ballooning weight. He had shot up to 224 pounds and was photographed looking every inch a slob rather than a superstar. Despite talk of his love of junk food, Jack was, he promised, on a strict diet. 'I suddenly realized that I had maybe 15, 20 years left and I was fat and bloated and looking like a beagle on downers. I saw where I was headed and it didn't look pretty. I'm not anxious to imitate Marlon Brando.'

Whether his appearance was to blame or not is uncertain, but just one month later it was revealed that Rebecca had dumped him for a man of 32, film-maker

Above: A scene from *Hoffa*, directed by Danny DeVito, left. Jack's portrayal of the American Teamsters union boss who vanished without trace in 1975 amid rumors of a Mafia murder, was widely considered to be one of his best performances. 'I didn't just act Jimmy Hoffa, I became him,' recalled Jack.

Right: This publicity shot was used to promote *Hoffa* and featured both Jack and DeVito. The two men had appeared together in *One Flew Over The Cuckoo's Nest* over a decade previously.

Jonathan Silverman. But it seems more likely that she did not want to find herself in Anjelica Huston's situation. She complained that Jack's tendency to ring her late at night to come over because he wanted sex was 'just plain insulting,' and said she had found a man to whom she was more than a mere sex toy. Cobras, like leopards it seems, do not change their spots. Jack had also been dating 22-year-old French model, Julie Delpy. At first Jack was outraged, and there was talk that he had pulled out of investing $6 million of his own money to launch Rebecca's film career in *Blue Champagne*. Within weeks he began repeating his lifelong pattern of trying to win his woman back. He told journalists: 'I realized that by carrying on in my old ways I was making her insecure. And that wasn't fair because she's a wonderful woman. While we were apart I realized how much I missed her, the kids and a proper home life. Heck, they'd given me roots I didn't realize I needed. Who wants to fool around when you've got a solid gold base? It's all a matter of what's more important – high living or good loving.' On this occasion his Irish gift of the gab doesn't seem to have worked and, according to the latest reports, he was consoling himself with dinner dates with a number of female friends, including British former 'wild child' Amanda de Cadenet. He was also said to have a crush on model Rennee Jeffus, notable for her work for Levi jeans.

His pain may have been slightly eased by the public's reception to *Hoffa*. Critics were unanimous in their praise, calling it a 'powerhouse of a performance,' although the Oscar went instead to Al Pacino for *Scent Of A Woman*. At the time of writing, Jack had

Above: Jack pictured with actress Lyndall Hobbs at the 1993 Academy Awards. Unfortunately he didn't win an Oscar either for *A Few Good Men* or for *Hoffa*.

accepted a staggering $5 million to appear in an epic love story, *Wolf*, playing opposite Michelle Pfeiffer, to be directed by Mike Nichols. He was also said to be interested in starring as Tom Cruise's gay lover, in an as yet untitled film that was once intended to have been made with Paul Newman and Robert Redford. Many actors would be nervous of such a role, but Jack presumably thinks his heterosexual credentials are safely established.

At 55 Jack is the ultimate Hollywood survivor. He has starred in some brilliant movies, and in some turkeys. But he knows how to bounce back: even when his love life was in shreds he still managed to produce a performance like the one given in *Hoffa*. Jack is fabulously rich – conservative estimates put his worth at well over $100 million – and does not feel remotely guilty about it. Some say he still rues the day that he lost Anjelica, and that there's nothing sadder than a middle-aged playboy chasing after young women and trying to recapture his lost youth. Yet, to his credit, no one can accuse him of 'withering dismally with age,' in the words of his favorite fellow-Irishman, James Joyce.

Above: Jack is always co-operative in promoting his movies. Here he is seen leaving Los Angeles to fly to Paris for the European opening of *Hoffa*.

Right: Jack pictured on location in Greenwich Village, New York, while making the new Mike Nichols film, *Wolf*, with Michelle Pfeiffer.

FILMOGRAPHY

1958: *Cry Baby Killer*

1960: *Too Soon To Love*
The Little Shop Of Horrors
The Wild Ride
Studs Lonigan

1961: *The Broken Land*

1963: *The Raven*
The Terror
Thunder Island

1964: *Back Door To Hell*
Ensign Pulver

1965: *Flight To Fury*
Ride The Whirlwind

1966: *The Shooting*

1967: *The St Valentine's Day Massacre*
Hell's Angels On Wheels
The Trip

1968: *Head*
Psych-Out

1969: *Rebel Rousers*
Easy Rider

1970: *On A Clear Day You Can See Forever*
Five Easy Pieces

1971: *A Safe Place*
Carnal Knowledge
Drive, He Said

1972: *The King Of Marvin Gardens*

1973: *The Last Detail*

1974: *Chinatown*
The Fortune

1975: *Tommy*
The Passenger
One Flew Over The Cuckoo's Nest

1976: *The Missouri Breaks*
The Last Tycoon

1978: *Goin' South*

1980: *The Shining*

1981: *The Postman Always Rings Twice*
Reds
The Border

1983: *Terms Of Endearment*

1985: *Prizzi's Honor*

1986: *Heartburn*

1987: *The Witches Of Eastwick*
Broadcast News
Ironweed

1989: *Batman*

1990: *The Two Jakes*

1992: *Man Trouble*
A Few Good Men
Hoffa

INDEX

Film titles are italicized
Page numbers in italics indicate
illustrations

Acknowledgments

The publisher would like to thank Mike Rose for designing this book, Clare Haworth-Maden for editing it, Nicki Giles for production, and Helen Jarvis for compiling the index. The following individuals and agencies provided photographic material:

Allsport USA/photograph, Vince Bucci: page 85
Allsport USA/photograph, Ken Levine: page 84
The Bettmann Archive: pages 24, 26 (both), 30, 54
British Film Institute: pages 12-13, 14, 15 (both), 16 (both), 17, 18, 19
Brompton Books: pages 1, 2-3, 4-5, 6, 7, 9, 11 (left), 20-21, 22-23, 27, 28-29, 32 (both), 33, 35 (bottom), 36 (top), 37, 38-39, 40, 41, 42-43, 44, 45, 46 (both), 47, 49, 50-51, 56, 57 (top), 58 (both), 59, 60, 61 (top), 62-63, 64-65, 66, 67 (top), 68 (top), 69, 71, 72 (both), 73, 76, 77, 78, 86 (both), 87, 89 (both), 91
Brompton Books/photograph, François Duhamel: page 90
Brompton Books/photograph, Elliott Marks: page 8 (bottom)
Brompton Books/Movie Star News: pages 25, 34, 36 (bottom), 52, 61 (bottom), 79
Brompton Books/Movie Star News/ photograph, Elliott Marks: page 81 (top)
Alec Byrne, Hollywood: pages 10 (both)
Ron Galella, New York: pages 55 (both), 57 (bottom), 70
Ron Galella, New York/photograph, Robert Ortega: page 83
Ron Galella, New York/photograph, Anthony Salignano: pages 82 (bottom), 88, 93
Ron Galella, New York/photograph, James Smeal: pages 80, 82 (top), 92 (both)
UPI/Bettmann Newsphotos: pages 31 (both), 35 (top), 48, 53, 62 (top left), 67 (bottom), 68 (bottom), 74-75